"Leslie Short provokes a dialog that must be had in every board room, every C-Suite, every organization, every home. Her ability to honor the resilience of anyone who has experienced exclusion and diagnose the illness it causes is powerful. Her ability to tackle the disease head on with surgical precision, find the root cause and extract it, has the ability to heal us all. Heed her words, they will forever change you."

— **Kim Smith**, Global Vice President, IBM

Expand Beyond Your Current Culture is a boot camp guide on how to have a diverse and inclusive work environment. It is an easy and frank read, and if you put in the work, you and your company will come out wiser and more powerful.

— **Michele J. Bianco**, Managing Director & Associate General Counsel, Americas Head of Prime Brokerage Legal/GBAM

"The book is a must-read for anyone who is serious about helping move the needle on Diversity and Inclusion. As Leslie mentions in her introduction, she wrote the book 'as if you and I were sitting in a café or bar, having a conversation on what's working in your organization and what isn't.' What her introduction fails to mention is that it will be the most entertaining and informative café experience you've ever had, full of laughter and tears, gut-punches and brain-benders. The entire book is chock-full of very specific, practical advice, as well as many thoughtful points that will force you to put down the book and reflect on what you just read."

— **Paolo Gaudiano**, Co-founder, Aleria PBC

"Investing in 'getting it right' is at the heart of Expand Beyond Your Current Culture. Leslie does a masterful job of including real-life situations that highlight the importance of forward thinking in a way that protects your bottom line. Addressing D&I from an 'it's just good business' perspective takes away the uncomfort-able-ness of a company or project manager doing their due diligence on topics – race, culture, gender identity, etc. – that they would instinctively shy away from."

— **Phil Jones**, Senior Director, Lime

"Anyone can come up with brilliant ideas; only a few can bring ideas along with thorough execution steps/plans. Without that, ideas will just stay being 'ideas.' Obviously, steps were laid out clearly throughout this book on how Diversity and Inclusion can be achieved."

— **Grace Lee**, former Director of Asian Marketing, Remy Cointreau USA

Leslie's book is filled with information, tools, and relatable stories for you as a leader and your organization to take a realistic assessment of the culture while providing helpful steps to improve. It is a great source to keep your corporation on the right track or to begin your corporate journey of Diversity and Inclusion.

— **Sharon Price John**, President and CEO, Build-A-Bear Workshop

EXPAND BEYOND YOUR CURRENT CULTURE

EXPAND BEYOND YOUR CURRENT CULTURE

DIVERSITY & INCLUSION
FOR CEOS & LEADERSHIP

LESLIE SHORT

CONTENTS

ACKNOWLEDGEMENTS

Special thank you to my family for their support through every twist and turn of my many careers. Gothrie, Mae, Sheri, and Michael, I love you dearly!

———

Tony Rahsaan and Lynne Filderman, from the moment I said I'm opening the doors of The Cavu Group, you both said I'm in! Thank you!

———

Tony Rahsaan deserves an extra thanks for also creating the graphics in the book, social media content, and working on the book cover with the publisher. He's the only one who gets away with calling me and simply saying, NO, that doesn't work!

———

Stanley Desbas, thanks for the photo shoot that is now being used as my promo.

———

Anne Hegeman, thanks for your publishing insights and for your unwavering friendship throughout the years.

———

Becca Lee, thank you for allowing me to use your poem in the book. I hope that nobody ever feels they need to apologize for their space at home or at work.

ACKNOWLEDGEMENTS

To all the participants who took the time to fill out the questionnaire, I am forever grateful for your time and honesty. Thanks to those who called, texted, and emailed stories to add to the book.

———

To all of my friends who supported me through the writing of the book, and for those of you who had special jobs during the writing of the book, you deserve an extra thank you. I cannot name you all, but please know I appreciate all of my friendships, champions, advocates, and allies!

———

Dwayne Andrews, my unofficial-official attorney, thank you for jumping in and always ensuring that I do more than check the boxes when it comes to my business deals.

———

To The Cavu Group Council, thank you for sharing your knowledge.

———

Finally, Jim at Maven Press, for saying "I didn't think about you being black." You had something to say about a topic that needs to be discussed. Thank you!

LS

A Note to CEOs and Leadership

I'M NOT ONE TO MINCE WORDS or, as the saying goes, I'm not a banana-up-the-tailpipe kind of woman. Let's put it on the table and figure it out, whatever it is. We can figure it out if we want to.

All the careers I've had have led me to focus on Diversity and Inclusion full time, and that's how my company The Cavu Group was born. To be effective and to be part of the process of change, I've also had to bring in my mediation, pastoral care, conflict-coaching, and leadership skills to support that focus. There are a lot of feelings and nuances in implementing a successful Diversity and Inclusion effort, even if folks don't want to admit it.

For some reason the concept of Diversity and Inclusion (D&I) is a floating cloud that everyone is trying to grab hold of. Why? Because we're told to make it happen. Or we know that we need to do it. Or we genuinely understand how the world works.

If you're stuck dealing with Diversity and Inclusion, or you're not sure that you have it covered, this book is for you. It's a simple read, and it will guide you with honest answers from over 30 people who are a mix of gender, race, religion, disabilities, and LGBTQ+. They represent, but are not limited to, tech, education, theater, writing, fashion, art, automotive, disability activism, medical, media, financial services, sales, events, promotions, construction, risk management, photography and video, lobbying, public relations, not-for-profits, social media, marketing, the faith community, entertainment, wellness, travel, personal and executive development, communications, architecture, engineering, science, service industry and the C-suite. I didn't want to write a book from only my perspective; I wanted to share with you how people under different parts of the diversity umbrella feel and think.

Throughout the book you'll see quotes from these participants. Please don't assume, if you see the same title under different quotes, that they're from the same person or that you can guess who they are.

I've written the book as if you and I were sitting in a café or bar, having a conversation on what's working in your organization and what isn't, and, most of all, how the diverse community that you're supposed to be focusing on knows whether your commitment to Diversity and Inclusion is real or not.

Those of you who are part of that diverse community can give this book as a gift to those you feel need to know the real deal on Diversity and Inclusion though you may not be able to talk to them about it yourself. I hope I've done that for you.

Read this book, and continue to use it as a reference today and in the future. And let's chat when you've finished.

— Leslie Short

UNDERSTAND WHY

YOU DO
THE THINGS
YOU DO

CHAPTER 1

What's In Your Bag?

W HEN I TRAINED TO BECOME A CERTIFIED MEDIATOR, one of the first questions the teacher asked was: "What's in your bag?"

People in the room looked at each other, wondering: What is this teacher talking about? He then asked, "How are you going to help others find their footing if you don't understand why you do the things you do?"

That stuck with me. There are so many people who have good intentions, and who want to be fixers, yet don't have the interpersonal tools or self-understanding to help and not hurt.

It's the same challenge with Diversity and Inclusion. How can you demand that Diversity and Inclusion be an initiative for your company when you haven't thought about what you bring to the organization as a leader and how you'll help the initiative be successful?

You'll most likely need to read and reread and reread the paragraph below. If it's confusing, it's because some of you try to make Diversity and Inclusion confusing. It's not!

> Listen, if you're looking at *diversity* as They & Them and *inclusion* as once they're in the company they're in, but not really We & Us, then you need to examine your culture and your thoughts about They & Them and We & Us and why you think that way.

We all have biases. Being aware of your biases, and understanding why you carry them in your bag, will allow you to work toward getting past the biases and controlling them when they pop up.

For example, we've all seen news stories about people who scream at others to speak English. America has an abundance of cultures and cultural offerings. So, when someone demands that someone else speak only English, you need to understand that the story is about the screamer, not the screamed-at.

When was the last time you had to step outside of your comfort zone? Are you comfortable with socializing outside of your comfort culture, outside of work? Outside of a company function? When was the last time you were where a different language was spoken, or the food was different? At a restaurant? Or out of the country?

If your vacation is where you last heard a language other than English, that doesn't count! That's because you knew it was for a limited time, and you could go back to your comfort culture and share how great the vacation was with your friends and make everyone listen to the new phrases you learned in a new language. But if you heard that foreign language in your office, you might tell the speaker that it's not wise to speak in their native tongue.

But the people in your company are not They & Them, and you're not on vacation where you can just walk away. They & Them are now We & Us in the company, and if you don't realize that, you need to dig deeper into your bag and check for bias. Understanding cultural differences should be part of the company culture.

I get that we carry lots of stuff in our bags, especially if we live in a city and don't drive to work. Many of us carry stuff that others can't see, and that's what we need to examine. Be clear that I'm not just putting this on leadership – together we must check our bags and see what's accumulated in them from childhood, from college, from adulthood. Things get lost and things get added. Make sure that you take the time to dump everything out of your bag so that you know what you're carrying.

When you have a better understanding of what's important to you, how you communicate, and why you do the things you do, then you can view others in the same light you want to be viewed in.

Leadership and Diversity

Holding a leadership position doesn't make you a leader. Your walk, your talk, and your actions make you a leader. Anyone can be a boss, but understanding how to add diverse cultures into a workplace takes a leader.

I'm using the words *diverse* and *diversity*, but if you've ever heard me speak you know that I don't like them because they're so easily tossed around. We're all diverse. I don't care if you have the same skin color or not, we're diverse in our thinking, walking, working, and all that's in our bags – what we bring to the workplace.

The idea that you can check your bag when you arrive at work, the way you would check your luggage at the airport, is a lie! You know darn well that when you get to work some of the stuff you try to shove to the bottom of your bag floats or jumps up, because that's who you are and how you act.

When someone's in a good mood, everyone knows that today is a good day, or this moment is a good moment, to work with them. If they're not in a good mood, then folks know that today is not the day. We carry these feelings in our bags, and that's one element of company culture. I'm not saying it's a good element; I'm saying it's an element that you need to be aware of.

If leadership doesn't make diversity a foundation of the company's culture, it won't work.

Unconscious Bias

What Is Unconscious Bias?

It's thinking that you just don't like something but you're not sure why. You're prejudiced against something, someone, some group and you're unaware of it. The bias could be based on race, ethnicity, gender, age, socio-economic status, religion, sexual orientation, and so on.

Why Does Unconscious Bias Matter?

Unconscious bias matters because the status quo that's not inclusive is no longer acceptable. It's not OK to say you're sorry, you didn't know, when bias is being seen by everyone else but you. It is OK to ask questions when you don't know. Unconscious bias matters because it excludes certain people from taking part, certain people from being candidates for jobs, and diverse thinking in any situation. If you allow a bias to rule your choices, then you keep yourself, and your company, from growing.

How Can Unconscious Bias Be Combatted?

Everyone has unconscious biases. What's important is that you become aware of them and understand how you react to them.

I give people a simple quiz to test their bias. Before one woman took my quiz, she told me that there was no way she was biased; after the quiz she said she had to do better. She had no idea that she was biased and how her bias affected her life and her thoughts.

When you're aware of your biases you do better, or at least you can take a breath and ask yourself: Why am I making this decision? Have I looked at this issue through another lens?

Black Lives Matter? Is It bias?

No, it's not! When people get upset by the phrase and say *All Lives Matter* – I agree! All lives do matter! But when the conversation is about black lives, and black suffering, it's important to acknowledge that we're talking about black lives, not all lives, *Black Lives Matter* – period! Just as, in discussing the coronavirus pandemic, it's important to acknowledge that it's not the Asian flu. Be clear that each conversation is important, but different, and that each one needs to be heard.

They & Them

How do you think it feels to come to work each day not knowing what people are saying about you? How do you think it feels to wonder if people think that you're only there because of the color of your skin, or your gender, or you're a checked box?

Answer: You feel like you don't belong. It doesn't mean that people aren't nice to you or that your work isn't good; it means that you're left out of conversations and decision-making.

You show up and hope to be noticed and heard and respected for what you bring to work. No matter what department you're in, you want to be part of We & Us.

It's up to leadership to dig down into their bags and see what's in them before they try to help They & Them join We & Us.

Takeaways

1. Take time to be honest with yourself and review what you bring to work in your bag. How can you welcome others to join We & Us in the company?

2. Examine what We & Us means to you and to the company.

3. People want to be seen, heard, and respected and to feel that they're part of the big picture. If you're part of the organization's leadership then this is your responsibility. What will you do?

4. Can you keep your biases and be successful?

5. If you keep your biases up front and out in the open, what's your value to the company. How long will that be OK?

6. What are your real thoughts and feelings on women in the workplace? African American men and women in the workplace? Latino men and women? (I say men and women because companies look at men and women who are African American or Latino differently.) Asians? Those with disabilities seen and unseen? LGBTQ+?

7. Are you prepared to hire a transgender person and assure that they're treated as equals?

8. Are you prepared to have the difficult conversations needed for change? If you're not, are you ready to admit it and bring in someone who can?

9. Are you ready to be the *ripple in the pond of change* (to speak up about Diversity and Inclusion)?

10. You *do* see color, so stop saying you don't.

Ask Yourself

Who are you?

_____

_____

_____

_____

_____

_____

_____

_____

Who are They & Them?

_____

_____

_____

_____

_____

_____

_____

_____

_____

_____

WHAT'S IN YOUR BAG
THAT YOU
DON'T SEE COLOR?

YOU NEED TO
RECOGNIZE IT
BEFORE YOU CAN
FIX IT!

STOP SAYING YOU
DON'T. WE ALL DO!

NOT SEEING
COLOR IS A
FORM
OF BIAS AND
PRIVILEGE!

**I DON'T
SEE COLOR**

RACE IS JUST
RACE UNLESS
YOU DEFINE
ME BY IT!

YOU ARE NOT HELPING BY
PRETENDING NOT
TO SEE COLOR!

AREN'T WE ALL
THE SAME?

WHAT DOES DIVERSITY & INCLUSION MEAN TO YOU?

TO YOUR COMPANY?

CHAPTER 2

Does Diversity and Inclusion Matter to You?

To Your Company?

NOW THAT WE TOOK A MOMENT to examine what's in your bag. what do you bring to the table in the D&I space? What do you offer as a leader? What does Diversity and Inclusion mean to you?

Should you be thinking about Diversity and Inclusion as a leader? Is it part of the company policy, which means part of your job? Diversity and Inclusion isn't just a trend, so you'll need to figure out how to make it part of the company culture. Not rocking the boat no longer works.

If you answered yes to the questions above, but you feel that Diversity and Inclusion is more than policy and that you need to set an example, then what does that look like? If Diversity and Inclusion matters to you personally, how do you translate that into your work and into your department? You have to be careful that you're not creating siloed department goals and culture but that you're working to change your company goals and culture. (We'll cover that in more detail later in the book.)

Before we go further, let's break down the four pillars of We & Us to insure that, as you continue reading, we're on the same page. In addition to *diversity* and *inclusion* we add *equity* and *authentic company culture.*

The Four Pillars of We & Us

Diversity: Gender, race, LGBTQ+, disabilities – When I speak of diversity those are at the heart of the conversation; diversity includes more than gender and race. Some organizations also include veterans as part of the conversation, but I don't.

> *I was called out by a veteran for not adding veterans when I speak about diversity. I explained to him that I don't believe veterans should be included under diversity, and that I feel that veterans are sometimes included because companies don't think clearly about it. (By the end of our conversation he agreed with me.) Some companies receive extra benefits by hiring veterans, but what does that have to do with diversity? I'll share a story from that veteran later.*

Inclusion: We feel included when we're invited into the room and are introduced to at least two people, and we're not left to fend for ourselves.

> *Belonging is not the same as inclusion. You belong to a group. Inclusion is a feeling you have that you are welcomed into a space and are valued in that space.*

Equity: This means having access – being able to use the tools, promotions, training, and staff that are available to everyone else.

It's what keeps me invested in the company.

Company Culture: The feeling of walking into the office and knowing that we're doing the work we say we're doing.

We're heard, seen, and valued.

Review the four pillars, and ask yourself if they matter to you. And how do you make sure that they matter to others?

If the four pillars matter to you, then as a leader you need to insure that they matter to the company. If there isn't a commitment to these pillars, a real commitment, then you need to hold your company to task, because it's important! Saying it and doing it are two different things.

If you believe in the four pillars, and you execute them in your department but the rest of the company doesn't follow suit, then people in other departments feel that they're losing out. This is what I call department inclusion.

A manager proudly told me that his department is inclusive because he can control who gets hired, and he makes it a point to reach outside the company to find employees. I asked whether the rest of the company works the same way, and he said that he had no idea, but he's good! I told him that I applaud his actions, but that when he leaves the company his culture goes with him. Department culture isn't sustainable; company culture is.

When was the last time you reviewed your company policies, procedures, and mission statement? Look at them again, and you may find that diversity, inclusion, equity, and company culture aren't as important to your company as you thought.

When a company has made a commitment to expand beyond its current culture, its leaders constantly review company policies and procedures. If they don't review them, they can't ensure that new employees will understand the company culture or that they'll feel included. Who you are and what you stand for determine what your employees, as well as your customers, expect of you.

Once you've thought about the four pillars, and asked yourself if you're actively championing them, look in your bag. Ask yourself why you took your job. Then you'll realize that others at your company may have taken their jobs for the same reasons.

Additional Questions to Consider

- Why would anyone want to work here?
- What are we offering them in addition to the job?
- What keeps them here?
- How do we insure that they keep learning as we keep growing?

- How do we communicate the four pillars to them?

- How do we communicate them on a daily basis?

- How do we insure that we all live our mission statement?

- Who will insure that we keep checking in with staff? (This is not the job of Human Resources.)

- Do we have diversity outreach? If so, what is it? Does it make sense to our mission? Is it working? If so, why? If not, why not?

Inclusive Committees

If everyone on a committee looks like you, talks like you, and comes from a similar background as you, then you've formed a club, not a committee. Take the time to mix up your committee with people from various departments and cultural backgrounds. Don't have only leadership lead the committee or the meetings – give a voice to those who may be more comfortable sharing their discomfort with those outside of leadership. (This leads us into the topic of having a champion, an advocate, and an ally. I'll break down the differences below.)

Once a committee is formed, and it looks diverse and sounds diverse, you may hear things you may not want to hear. There will be discomfort before there's comfort (and maybe the committee will never really be comfortable). You have to ask again how important diversity, equity, inclusion, and authentic company culture are to your company. If you say that you're committed to do what's needed to assure an inclusive company culture, and to make it part of your foundation, then and only then will the real work begin.

Looking at your biases and differences is uncomfortable, but you need to be honest with each other to have a solid foundation and meaningful outreach. Ask yourself and others why it's important to have a committee made up of people from various departments and backgrounds so you have cultural understanding. Make sure you understand before you assume that everything is good.

Your Role

What will be your role in the process of building an inclusive workspace? Will you be a champion, an advocate, or an ally? What's the difference?

Champion: You bring up the issues when They & Them aren't in the room because it benefits the big picture.

Advocate: This is truly part of your DNA. You believe that We & Us is the only way to move forward as a collective group. You also make sure that We & Us is threaded throughout all initiatives in the company.

Ally: You can't call yourself an ally – that badge must be given to you. It's given to you once it's known that you rise to a situation regardless of what it is. We need to see that you're really about the work not because you have to be but because it's important and you hear us and see us and you move with us for us. It's not about you, and it's not a one-answer-fits-all. It's not logical, and it means traveling a road that may not have been traveled yet. You bob and weave with us.

————

When Being an Ally Is in Your DNA

In the 80s I was dancing on a cruise ship. It was in the days when cruising was a luxury. The ships had one dinner seating and were full of iconic Hollywood movie stars and the elite of the elite. The shows that were produced for the ships were like Broadway shows, with dancers, singers, and a live orchestra.

I was one of those dancers and the first black dancer to ever work on the cruise ship in any position. Before I was allowed to join the ship, I had to be approved by the corporate office in Norway. There were some who weren't sure how the elite passengers would react to a black dancer. As dancers we also hosted dinner tables with the guests and one of the activities during the cruise, such as ping pong or shuffleboard. So during the two-week cruise guests would see me on and off stage.

I should mention that I was also in charge of the other dancers. As the dance captain I had my own cabin and had to report to the on-shore office how things were going with the show and the dancers.

Before leaving Las Vegas, where we rehearsed for the show, the choreographer held a meeting to explain that I would be the first black person to be on the cruise as an employee. She wanted to prepare the other dancers to answer questions from passengers. Sure enough, one night at dinner one of the dancers, hosting his dinner table, was asked by a wealthy older white woman, "Why is she here? How did she get hired? Why is she in charge of the dancers?"

I wouldn't have known about the incident if I hadn't heard Ted's voice rise above his normal tone and then seen him leave the dining room. Later that night I asked him what had happened. He said, "How dare she ask those questions?" I reminded him of the talk we had before leaving and told him he didn't have to fight for me, to stay calm, that I would be OK. I told him that she asked what others might have been thinking.

Fast-forward twenty years – Ted and I are connected on Facebook. I saw a post about how saddened he was for black families having to teach their boys about the police and wonder if they would come home at night. He said that he never had to think about that when his sons walked out the door. Where was the fairness and justice in this, and how could he do better? How could he stand up?

I don't normally respond on Facebook, but I needed to remind Ted that he has always stood up and that writing about his feelings is a form of standing up. Ted is now teaching theater and is still fighting for justice. Being an ally is in Ted's DNA, and all these years later I still consider him one of my allies.

THERE'S MORE TO **DIVERSITY & INCLUSION** THAN CHECKED *BOXES*

CHAPTER 3

Checked Boxes Aren't Good Enough!

M ANY COMPANIES THINK that if they've checked the boxes described below they've followed the law and they've done all they need to do to be considered an equal opportunity employer. It should be clear to you after reading this chapter that companies can check the boxes without being seriously committed to Diversity and Inclusion.

Here are a few D&I boxes and, sadly, some real examples of the thinking of some companies in checking them:

☑ **Box 1 – Gender:** Try to find some women to join the board. Try to promote one or two. We only need one in the photo to say we're diverse.

☑ **Box 2 – Ethnicity:** Does Asian count? Or should we get one black person to insure that "others" see that we're diverse?

☑ **Box 3 – Race:** If you bring in the African American make sure they're not too black, you know, militant . . .

☑ **Box 4 – Sexual Orientation:** We can't ask if they're LGBTQ+, but if you find someone who screams it, make sure they're front and center. Not sure if we're ready for someone who's Trans. Let's hold onto that thought and just get one or two.

☑ **Box 5 – Disability:** Do we have the budget to hire someone with a disability? What happens if they need something our other employees don't? If you can find one who doesn't need much, then great.

☑ **Box 6 – Veteran:** We'll look really good if we have a veteran or two. Go to a job fair to find some.

☑ **Box 7 – Age:** Age isn't a mandatory box, and we can't ask how old they are, so if they look too old we can just say they're not the right company culture fit.

☑ **Box 8 – Personal Attribute:** We can't hire a heavy female – they won't fit our image.

☑ **Box 9 – Religion:** It might be difficult to find a Muslim to hire. Maybe someone Jewish (not as noticeable).

You get the point. And I'm not making these up – I've heard all of them in meetings!

Once these boxes have been checked, which covers the company by law, they'll usually do the following: 1) State on their website that they're an equal opportunity employer; 2) Make it part of their application process; 3) Tell HR to make a diversity effort.

I've heard it said in some companies, "It's not that serious, but why cause issues? Let's cover our asses just in case someone notices." The funny thing is, these companies believe they're an equal opportunity employer.

Be careful of your checked boxes. Companies have asked me how potential employees (or customers) would know whether they are or aren't committed to Diversity and Inclusion. The answer is obvious – they clearly state that they're an equal opportunity employer on their website! (And, yes, that's sarcasm.)

Before people apply for a job with your company, or during the hiring process, here are a few ways They can tell that you don't really have a diverse culture (let alone an inclusive one.)

- You use stock photos on your website to show that you're diverse, but you've used the same photos that other companies are using.

- They're told before they arrive to maybe shorten their name.

- You ask Them, "Do you have an American name? One that's easier to pronounce?"

- You've recruited Them for a job They didn't apply for, and told Them that you got their name "through research." (Don't you really want to say that you reached out to your diverse contacts to receive additional resumes?)

- You asked Them, "Would you be comfortable working here?"
- You told Them that They may want to tone it down for the interview or the second interview.
- They walk into the office and see no one who looks like Them or to any "other" culture.
- During the interview, They consistently hear the words *they* and *them*.
- They see that there's no diverse leadership in your company.
- On the tour of your company They still don't see anyone who looks like them.
- If They do see someone who looks like Them, They're told, "I'm sure you and _____ (fill in the blank) will have a lot in common."

Let's say you're purposefully diversifying your company. You've checked several boxes and you're trying to check a few more, but no one can tell. Your responses to the questions below are just a few ways people will know whether you're checking the boxes or not.

- How do you train your employees?
- Do you pair employees with someone who's been in the company for some time to help them maneuver through the system for the first month?
- How do you handle inviting employees to meetings and introducing them?

- What type of outside projects and events does your company sponsor?

- What types of people do you like to work with?

- Do you have cultural initiatives?

- How do you describe your company culture?

- How do you create an inclusive environment?

- How do you support personal and professional development?

- Is your website accessible?

What About Human Resources?

Let's take a few steps back to the checked boxes. Where were these employees found so that the boxes could be checked off ? Job fairs? Schools? Clubs? Sororities? Fraternities? Ads offering employee incentives? Job placement boards?

I want to be clear that I'm not beating up on human resources professionals on how they find employees. I work with them a great deal, so I understand what they're up against. They take direction from higher-ups in the company. Who's giving them direction? How much support do they get to use unconventional resources to find someone who fits many of the boxes?

Several HR specialists have told me that they were asked to find diverse candidates to interview, but when they submitted those candidates there were always "issues." Things that make you wonder. I guess the fact that HR tried is a box that gets to be checked off.

Large companies can afford to have their HR departments use artificial intelligence (AI) or computer programs that recognize buzzwords – oops, I mean targeted keywords or phrases to search for employees. It's lucky for them that they can afford the software or a company to handle their search, but it's not so lucky for the job-seekers who may not have gone to the college or have the degree that was programmed into the computer as a requirement for employment (unbeknownst to the job-seeker). Of course, these computer programs introduce all kinds of bias into the hiring process.

Story Time

This is a good time to share the story from the veteran I mentioned in the last chapter.

> My experience has been very different as a veteran coming out of the service, after twelve years, into the workforce. As I started that journey, I realized I had two checks in the box for diversity – being African American and being a veteran. But I didn't want those two factors to be the only reasons why someone would hire me. I felt that I needed to show the workforce that I'm qualified and I'm not your average veteran who left the military with no game plan.
>
> I remember the day I went to a job recruiter and she told me that I wasn't real! I was perplexed for a second, and then she explained herself. She said that there was no way that I was able to be in the military, complete bachelor's

and master's degrees, work a second job, and have my own business when we all have the same twenty-four hours in a day. It doesn't seem real! I was surprised by her comment. I left the office feeling very discouraged. Were my qualifications not what companies were looking for? Was I overqualified for the positions I was applying for?

The interaction I had with that recruiter pushed me into the world that I was destined to be in, which is fashion. I'm now in a position to move to the beat of my own drum while still learning the essential skills that are needed to be successful in the fashion industry.

— Former U.S. Navy Chief/
Creative Director Fashion

A New Box

I hope you realize that as you're evaluating a potential employee's added value, they're evaluating the value you bring to them.

Here's a new box for you – my box. Didn't think about that, did you? What does that even mean?

People who walk into your company may have more than one box to check. Someone may be biracial and a veteran, or Asian and a woman. Do you just pick the box that works for you and not take the effort to see who they are? Are you just happy that you found one person who checks several boxes so that you're covered?

That doesn't work. Checking the box is only as good as checking the box, which means nothing. Checking the box is not good enough! Unless you make an effort to hire the people who are best for the position, the ones who have the talent and not just the exterior that lets you check the box, then you're making an empty gesture. If you already know this, please share it with others in leadership, because some of them still don't understand valuing talent over checked boxes. They point fingers and say that pushing D&I doesn't make sense. But others can point to the bottom line that says it makes sense to hire for talent, and if boxes are checked that's great.

You have to make the effort to insure that equity is a top priority, remembering that equity equals access. People need the opportunity to grow within the company, to see that it's possible to grow within the company. They need to learn new skills, they need to know where they can find the information that enables them to do that, they need to know who they can speak to who will hear them and see them and guide them.

That good feeling of inclusion. The same feeling you wanted when you took the job.

Some Sad Examples

It's clear that the way companies have been approaching D&I isn't working, and just checking boxes isn't good enough. Just take a look at some real-life examples that will make you cringe.

The following products should never have been approved to reach the public:

- Blackface sweaters
- Monkey sweatshirts
- Sambo charms
- Anti-anything shirts or jackets
- Clothing that appears to be concentration camp uniforms ...

And companies have engaged in the following atrocious behaviors:

- Refusing to allow certain people to sit in their coffee shop
- Storing a wheelchair improperly during travel
- Telling someone to take off their head scarf
- Cutting someone's hair in the middle of a competition
- Stopping same-sex kissing
- Not having a clean area to use a breast pump
- Told there is no ramp – sorry, but you can't go there
- Taking a photo in a diverse country without one diverse person in the photo while saying you're there for diversity ...

If you aren't familiar with any of these stories – that too is an issue.

Sorry? Not Really

I keep wishing that companies would learn from each other, but they don't seem to. A company hits the news for doing something that's blatantly racist, but the next week another company does the same thing, and on and on.

Just saying "Sorry" is no longer acceptable. In today's world we *expect* companies to do better and to have a diverse and inclusive company culture. So if all you do is check the boxes, and those in leadership positions aren't committed to D&I, and all you do is keep saying you're sorry, then customers will take their business elsewhere.

We know companies that have diversity, inclusion, and authentic company culture as part of their foundations, and have introduced products that represent their full range of customers. They have invested in various communities. They show up, they speak out, and they stand true to their purpose and mission. And if they misstep, they address that misstep with a viable plan, a real plan, not a plan to just quiet things down. Not just say they're sorry.

Yes, we can tell the difference. #imsorryisbroken

So, your boxes are checked – now what?

DIVERSITY & INCLUSION
SHOULD BE A PROMISE WITH

EXECUTION

NOT

A PROBLEM
AND A PROMISE

CHAPTER 4

With Diversity and Inclusion Comes Responsibility

NOW THAT WE'RE CLEAR that saying sorry is no longer good enough, let's talk about what needs to happen so that you aren't in the position of having to repeat that you're sorry.

Diversity and Inclusion should be a promise with execution. That means the following:

1. If you say that you're a fair and just company, and that Diversity and Inclusion is part of your company culture, but it's on paper only, that's a promise to no one – it's only a statement.

2. When you make the promise, what does the promise mean?

3. How are you executing on that promise?

4. Look around your company. How diverse is it?

5. In what departments do you have diverse staff?

6. What type of diversity do you have?

7. Who is responsible for hiring ?

8. What's the background of those doing the hiring?

9. How do they approach hiring?

10. Where are you posting your job listings?

11. Who's writing the job listings?

12. What wording are you using in the listings?

13. Who's in the room when people are being interviewed? A diverse team would be nice to see, but only, and I do mean only, if they're in leadership roles or part of the D&I committee. Do not have someone of color, someone who's LGBTQ+, a woman, or a disabled person in the interview as props.

14. Don't place ads for a Head of Diversity and Inclusion if you're not planning to hire. If months later you still haven't hired anyone, and the ad is still running, then you're just pretending to keep your promise.

15. Does your promise include not only hiring for diversity but insuring that you make an effort to be inclusive?

16. Does inclusive mean more than just being in the room?

17. Whose voices are heard in the room?

18. Whose voices are asked to contribute to the conversation?

Ask yourself the above questions because they're the first step toward your company becoming diverse and inclusive. It sounds simple, but I've had CEOs tell me that they just don't know where to begin or what questions to ask. This is a beginning.

What You Need to Do

Let's jump ahead. You're about to hire people who will bring diversity into the company. If the company hasn't been diverse in the past, do you share your thinking with the present company employees? Do you explain the importance of bringing in different thoughts and outlooks for the success of the company? Do you let them know that the company is changing and growing and that you're invested in the change and growth?

***The answer to the above questions
should be obvious – Yes!***

Let's say that you've already implemented Diversity and Inclusion in your company, but some employees still feel that they aren't included or aren't treated fairly. After many meetings and approval from the board (if that's what's needed) you decide to create committees and announce to the company that you'll make changes.

The question becomes, have you listened to where the disconnect is coming from? Have you taken the time to speak with those in charge, and those not in charge, before you throw committees at the issue? Have you asked how the company can make the issue better? A company survey isn't the best way to find out what employees are thinking because, no matter what you say to the contrary, employees know that the responses can be tracked to the people who made them. Hold round-tables instead, with an outside consultant and which-ever leadership is most appropriate.

All too often, the kneejerk reaction is to promise change, make a half-hearted effort, and then say it didn't work. If you promise change, then make change. You have to keep making the effort to make change until you find what works.

Here's what you need to do:

1. Speak to the people who are disconnected and ask them what developments they would like to see to insure that their issues are addressed.

2. Ask the allies, champions, and advocates to oversee departments outside of their own, to be the key point people for those departments so that there's someone employees can approach. Every situation doesn't need to go to HR. In most situations an employee just needs someone to walk through an issue with them without judgment.

3. Training videos don't have the impact that comes from bringing someone in to interact with people. Bring in people who can relate to your staff and company culture, who can make people aware of what's actually going on.

4. Providing D&I training once a year isn't helpful. Training should be done before it's needed, not when it's mandatory.

5. Trainings and workshops that haven't been updated to include the faces of today's workers

won't have the impact that's needed. Remember that diversity is more than race and gender; it also includes LGBTQ+ and those with disabilities.

6. Bring in people who represent all groups, and make the point that your company wants to invest in creating a series of trainings that speak to the company culture. Then your employees will know that your promise isn't an empty promise but the foundation of the company.

7. Let employees know when new D&I laws have been passed and that you'll be updating the company handbook to insure that everyone is aware of the changes.

8. Before jumping into training, have someone come in and do a full D&I company assessment. When I do assessments I start from the moment I walk through the door. I look at when restrooms are cleaned, how the space makes me feel, who the people are, how staff speak to each other, and many other factors. CEOs have been shocked at what my assessments have revealed. After an assessment I determine what direction the company should take and what trainings they should engage in to insure the growth of the company and its employees. This takes up to a month, if not more.

9. Conflict coaching is an option to offer your employees to settle internal issues. Conflict coaching has grown out of mediation, and it's aimed

at working with those on one side of an issue. Often, when I've arrived to mediate a case, I've found that only one side would show up. Mediators cannot listen to only one side, so all I could do was reschedule. The side that didn't show up (for whatever reason) was left helpless, frustrated, and deflated. Of course, those who showed up walked out more frustrated then when they walked in. New York State has conducted a pilot program to train certified mediators to be conflict coaches, allowing mediation centers to offer the service when one side doesn't show up.

My job as a conflict coach is not to tell the party what to do but to help them see their options if the other side doesn't want to change. I help them see how to deal with their feelings and move forward.

Sometimes employees leave a meeting or a job because they were frustrated from not being heard or appreciated. Meeting with a conflict coach may allow them to see the situation in a different light and may show them how they also have to change if they want others to change.

———

Diversity and Inclusion is a two-way street. Each side needs to make an effort to understand the other.

———

Story Time

Allow me to share a personal story where D&I promises turned into a problem.

I was living and dancing in Paris, France (in my first career I was a professional ballet dancer). When I started, I danced for TV, film, and commercials. There were two other dancers of color at the time, but they were French; I was the only American black woman. I was the only black dancer on a popular TV variety show. The other dancers had issues with me being hired and being the lead dancer and dance assistant. In my mind that was their issue, not mine.

I knew what I needed for the show in regard to wardrobe – a dark brown or black wig and makeup to match my skin tone. I was told that the makeup artist would have what I needed; the wig was essential.

The day came for the final dress rehearsal. I went to pick up my wig and, guess what, there was no wig for me. They had decided, without speaking to me, that they just didn't have time to pick up the darker wig. We'd been rehearsing this show for two weeks, and the contract had been signed in advance. I had taken it upon myself, with the help of a French-speaking friend, to introduce myself to wardrobe, hair, and make-up in advance so that they would know that I was there (just in case my contract agreements hadn't made it to the folks who do the work). I was told oops, sorry, it just didn't happen. But sorry wasn't good enough. I picked up my dance bag and found the choreographer. I told him that he just lost his lead dancer because a promise wasn't kept. I had done my part to insure that wardrobe knew I was there and what I needed, and they decided it wasn't worth the effort.

My allies, champions, and advocates came through in ways that I never expected. I knew that the choreographer would stand up for me since he pushed to get me hired on a show where there were only white dancers, and he created dance segments for me. But I had no idea that the star of the show had been watching rehearsals, heard what happened, and demanded that I not only have the wigs that I needed but that I would have my own hair and makeup team so that wouldn't happen again.

That was a promise that turned into a problem that turned into a solution that I hope stuck for any person of color who worked there after I left. I also hope that the story lives on for anyone from a diverse culture who works there so that they know they can stand up! They may be surprised how many people are in their corner.

———

Promises and problems go beyond the walls of the traditional workplace. The people running a church wanted to open their congregation to those outside their community, so they placed an ad asking for blacks or people of color to join them. The ad said that they would be paid in doughnuts and that they could take whatever was left after the coffee hour. Seriously, I haven't made this up.

- **Solution 1:** If you want to diversify your church, speak with someone in charge at a house of worship of a different faith. Attend one of their services and invite them to attend one of yours. This is a way to build trust, to learn about other faiths, and to bring people together.

- **Solution 2:** Invite someone to be a guest preacher or speaker.

_____

Someone who was partially hearing impaired needed a piece of equipment that would make voices clear when he used the phone. The company he worked for provided the equipment for him (which makes sense since that would make him a better employee). Everything was great until the company was sold and he was told that the equipment was no longer going to be available. He was given the option to stay, but without the equipment he needed to do his job. Someone in the company, sadly, thought this was OK.

_____

Then there are the difficulties that disabled people have when they fly. They make prior arrangements and are promised that what they need will be there when they need it. In one case a man was forced to crawl across the tarmac, up the stairs, and down the aisle of the plane because the promised equipment wasn't there. He had to repeat the process in reverse when the plane landed. In another case a woman's wheelchair was stored with the luggage and was broken during the flight. She had to sue to try to be reimbursed for the value of the chair.

_____

This story has happened to different people at different companies.

One employee did great work, was loyal, and was praised by her company. But she noticed that other employees were doing the same job but were paid more. She requested a meeting and was told that the others got paid more because they had degrees. So, she decided to get a degree, and after she got it she asked for a second meeting to discuss a raise or promotion. No raise, no promotion. So, she decided to leave. At the third meeting the company wanted to know, Why are you leaving the company?

Why are you leaving the company? Companies lose out when they lose good people. They lose good people when they don't let those people move up the ladder, just because their color, disability, or sexual preference doesn't fit the company culture.

———

If you hear that there's a D&I issue in your company, don't brush it under the table. Communication is key. Whether the issue is regarding race, gender, or someone being made to feel unwelcome, it needs to be addressed. You need to take the time, and face being uncomfortable to solve the problem.

> Diversity is not a simple calculus, it's a social exercise. It's an exercise on how to best harvest the value of differences in lived experiences, ethnicity, gender, religion, geography, age, socio-economic status, etc. . . . and convert it into more impactful and more valuable (tangible or

intangible) deliverables for the clients. Inclusion is about equality in power and not demographic integration that mainly defines diversity.

— *Biophara consultant*

———

See something, say something, do something!

If not you, then who?

———

STOP
FAKING IT
HOPING YOU
WON'T GET
CAUGHT

CHAPTER 5

Aspiration vs. Operation
Making Diversity and Inclusion a Reality

I'VE ASKED EMPLOYEES what happens inside their companies that makes them think their company is just faking it till it makes it or gets caught. Here are a few words that keep coming up (and the context in which they come up):

1. **Integrity** (My company seems to lack it.)

2. **Transparency** (What's really going on?)

3. **Respect** (Why can't they just acknowledge my work?)

4. **Inclusion** (Why is it that those in leadership are the only ones who seem to matter?)

5. **Representation** (It would be nice to see someone like me in leadership.)

6. **Acceptance** (I am who I am – why do I need to change my . . .?)

7. **Leadership** (Stop reading from the press release.)

8. **Tired** (Why do I have to teach and explain over and over again how to bring diversity into the company?)

Here's what I hear from employees in more detail:

On Integrity

I was surprised how many times this word came up and how many people, both diverse candidates for jobs and those with solid careers, felt that their companies lacked integrity. It's a word that's mostly used internally because customers wouldn't know about a company's lack of integrity unless it became public.

Advice for leadership: Always demonstrate integrity and demand it from others.

On Transparency

This word came up in regard to money and budgets, especially in not-for-profit companies. When someone follows the money trail, too often the money isn't what it's supposed to be or where it's supposed to be, especially when it comes to helping diverse communities.

Employees told me that they wished that management would say what they mean and say what they're looking for, instead of having them do the work and then being told that it's not going to work.

One CEO said it best – "I can't promise to be transparent because there are things I just can't share, but what I can promise is visibility." I thought that was a fair answer. It's up to the staff, then, to hold the company accountable to insure that visibility remains a top focus.

Advice for leadership: If you're looking to check boxes you can use the following statement:

> We're looking to diversify our company and we're making every effort to do so on all levels. We're starting out by insuring that we have diverse talent and voices working with us.

At least you're saying that you're working on it, which is different from saying that you have it. By *it* I mean at least one person from a culture different from yours, aka diversity.

On Respect

We all know that this means different things to different people. The majority of responses I received when I asked about this word were: "I want my work to be recognized, and I don't mean with an award (which would be nice, but . . .). I would like to know that what I contribute, big or small, makes a difference to the company as a whole."

Advice for leadership: Take a moment to say, "I see you, I see your work, and thank you." This will go a long way toward building respect.

On Inclusion

This means making a conscious effort to insure that people are integrated into the system, that they have a feeling of purpose and belonging. It sounds so simple, but apparently it's not. Companies love to *say* that they're inclusive. They produce ads that make it appear that way, but they use actors in the ads, not employees.

Employees aren't going to put on fake smiles and pretend that they're included in meetings or have equal opportunities. But the actors are paid to make it look that way. The companies may not be as diverse as the ads makes them seem, and their few diverse employees aren't always made to feel welcome or heard or seen or valued or respected.

Advice for leadership: Make a conscious effort to insure that your employees have a feeling of purpose and respect.

On Representation

Take a look at the advertising, marketing materials, and commercials that show diversity in your offices or meetings. (You know, those purchased photos on your website.) To be honest, you know that there are few people of diverse cultures sitting in those glass-front offices or leading meetings.

Advice for leadership: To be truly diverse, your company must be true to its word and be diverse and inclusive at every level.

On Acceptance

If I walk in the door and you ask me to change my hair, my dress, my speech, then why did you hire me?

Advice for leadership: People want to know that they can be their whole selves at work. Don't tell them to bring their whole selves to work and then say that you really only want half of their selves at work. You're asking for a lawsuit. Don't tell people that they can't wear their hair a certain way when it doesn't affect their talent, their safety, or their ability to do their job. Please refer to The Crown Act (Create a Respectful and Open World for Natural Hair).

On Leadership

The leadership at some companies read to the world what their public relations departments write, which is normally a big-picture overview. What's said often doesn't apply to those who aren't in leadership roles, yet it affects what they need to do to execute the work. This is a prime example of aspirational vs. operational: taking what the company aspires to and making sure that it's part of the daily operations.

Advice for leadership: One of my favorite sayings is: "Having the title of leader doesn't make you a leader – sometimes you're only a boss." Leadership needs to lead by example, not by title. And hopefully leadership will lead with integrity.

At least that's the way it should be.

On Being Tired

African Americans lead the charge saying that they're tired. They're tired of being in a company that asks for advice and then does the opposite of the advice they're given. They're tired of seeing blacks, Hispanics, and Asians in company ads when the company wants to wave the diversity flag, even though there may only be one of each in the company. They're tired of feeling like they have to be the teachers about everything black. They're tired.

Advice for leadership: Be fully committed to Diversity and Inclusion.

Story Time

Perception vs. Reality

As I was gathering information for this book, this story kept coming back to me, and I felt that this is where it should be told.

I was called by a headhunter when I was working at a company that gave me full freedom – I traveled, made decisions, and got checks cut and signed. The money was good, and I was able to work on projects that I was personally invested in. When the headhunter called I wasn't really interested. I was already receiving calls from lots of headhunters since my position at the company and the results of my work were very visible. I turned them down.

But when the headhunter told me the name of the company she was calling for, it piqued my interest – it was the only company I thought I would want to work for in-house rather than as a consultant. Once I said I was interested the ball started rolling, first with phone interviews, then with people flying to New York to meet me. I was told that they were looking for the next team of executives who would eventually take top leadership roles in the company. I loved the company, and I still do for the most part.

All the interviews went well. I was told that the company wanted to fly me to headquarters so that I could meet not only the leadership but also some of the staff, since I would work in various departments. I said that I would like to go back to Europe, and I was told that that was a possibility but that first the new team would rotate at headquarters to learn the company from the bottom up.

I was still excited about the opportunity and flew out to meet everyone. This interest in me felt a little off since I didn't see where any of my personal interests or knowledge would play into decision-making at the company. But I understood that they wanted me to learn from the bottom up and then learn about their international operations, so I was still excited. I came back to New York and got a call from the headhunter, who told me how excited everyone was to meet me and that I only had a few more calls and one more meeting before a hiring decision would be made. This process took approximately one year. Keep in mind that I loved where I was, and I wasn't 100 percent sold on the new company, so I wasn't stressed about taking the job.

The headhunter said that the company was opening an office in Miami, and would I want to head up the marketing department? I said no, that I'd already done that and I wanted something bigger than heading a marketing department. The company showed a little attitude to my response, but we continued on with the "next team to take over leadership" interviews. After two more calls and a final breakfast the formal offer came via a call from the department head who would mentor me through phase one.

We had a great call. At the end of the call the department head said that he had one more request. He said that I was high energy and knew a lot about the different departments, but he was worried that I would intimidate the current staff. He asked me to tone it down until I was in the system.

My response was the same as it would be today. I said that I was toned down in the interviews and if I needed to tone down to join the team then no thank you.

When I told the headhunter about this conversation she was pissed, but I told her that she had wasted my time and hers. I'd been who I am from day one. If everyone thought I was too strong during the interviews, they didn't need to call me back to keep moving forward.

As much as I thought that would be a great company for my next move, it wasn't! The company wanted a certain type of person, but then they felt that I was going to be more than they could control. Not handle, control. A perfect example of perception vs. reality.

Today this company does a great job empowering women customers, but they're also engaged in several lawsuits with their employees.

If you aren't truly committed to your cause, mission, and staff, your customers will eventually realize it.

They can tell when you use public relations to pretend to be what you're not. You need to be all in. Or admit that Diversity and Inclusion is new for your company, and that you may take a few wrong turns; ask your customers to support you as you commit to Diversity and Inclusion and step into new territory. Your company will gain nothing but respect and loyal customers as long as you keep moving forward with an authentic commitment.

At a past speaking engagement I was asked about the word *tolerance* and how it fits if a company is trying to commit to Diversity and Inclusion. I have tolerance for a company that's actively trying to make changes. But I have zero tolerance for a company that repeats the same mistakes and thinks no one will notice. I have no tolerance for companies that feel they need to tolerate Diversity and Inclusion. No human wants to be tolerated.

> D&I is the thing companies claim to strive for but often fall short. Valentino gets so much praise for the amount of models in color during fashion week. Yet there's no diversity in the actual business or creative teams.
>
> — *Fashion & Art Magazine executive*

———

If you want to be aspirational, be operational as well! Take care of your inside as well as your outside!

We are watching!

———

More Stories About
Aspiration vs. Operation

I was President of Marketing, Advertising & PR for the apparel company FUBU The Collection (FUBU stands for "For Us By Us"). When I took that job, old bosses and other associates in various corporate jobs and industries told me that I was making the biggest mistake of my career, for several reasons: 1) The four owners were black; 2) They had some Jewish guys behind them; 3) The owners were young; 4) They looked like thugs; 5) They weren't my type of people; 6) It was a fad (you know, hip hop).

I didn't know a hip from a hop. I had lived in Europe and Asia for over thirteen years, and I understood culture, people, and business. What I didn't know about hip hop culture I learned, and I adjusted when needed and set rules and policy when needed.

This was in 1997. At its peak the company had over $350 million worth of sales, domestic and international licenses, and we were traveling and being featured in interviews all over the world. The same people who said I was making the biggest mistake of my career were asking me for jobs. Companies in the fashion industry wanted a piece of what we were creating.

Here's where we get into *aspiration* vs. *operation*. We had celebrities and multicultural models in our ads. Many denim companies thought, hey, if it works for them it'll work for us. They put any black, bald guy with no shirt and his underwear hanging out of a pair of denim jeans in ads and slapped those ads in *Vibe,*

Source, and any other music magazine they thought black folks were reading. They aspired to be FUBU, but they didn't have a clue that it would take more than a bald guy in jeans to connect to a culture and be relevant to the industry.

———

How do you aspire to connect to a company and culture when your company doesn't look like the folks you're going to speak to?

I was working for a hot company that was doing exciting new things, and corporate America wanted to be part of the action. They knew enough to come speak to us, but instead of coming with someone who could actually make a deal, they grabbed any black guy who worked for them and told him to come to New York to meet with us. I'm not positive, but I bet they told their guy, "Come take this meeting because we don't have anyone senior enough who looks like the folks we're going to meet with." I don't blame the black guy for getting on a plane to New York so he could be in one of the hottest showrooms with a hot brand that was relevant to his culture (and to other cultures, just not to the folks arranging the meeting).

As everyone walked into the showroom we began introductions. The meeting was with a car company, although the company I was working for wasn't part of the automobile industry.

The guests from the car company introduced themselves, and the first four titles made sense to me: Marketing, Product Development, Sales, and a VP of

Partnerships. Then the one black guy, who they clearly hadn't prepped, says he's in seatbelts!?! He installed seatbelts. I knew then how the meeting was going to go. They were clueless. They were trying to jump into a culture that they thought they could make money from, without real research or thinking things through clearly.

Needless to say the conversation between our companies stopped after that meeting because I said to them on the way out that the next time it would be OK if they came to the table with their full selves and without a prop.

They aspired to be one thing, but operationally they weren't ready to make it a reality.

If you aspire to be part of cultural happenings, you need to do your research. Don't assume that any person will do to represent you, because then you're assuming that the people you're trying to reach are dumb and followers. Because you sold to them before doesn't mean you'll sell to them again.

———

Years ago you may have gotten away with this kind of behavior, but today customers and employees will hold your feet to the fire. We see you, so your operations need to match your aspirations. Pretending to be what you aren't won't work. That's what the right partnerships are for!

There are many black, Hispanic, Asian, disability, and LGBTQ+ agencies you can partner with that are doing amazing work, so do more research to discover them (not just the top five). Better yet, take the time to ask around about who's doing good, consistent work who can introduce you to new markets, old markets, and untapped markets.

If you're honest about aspiring to be part of new markets, then you have to show up for more than just the cultural holidays. You have to make true investments and commitments into those markets, and if you need help, then find the right agencies to help you.

Some Advice for Leadership

Your company has made the commitment to Diversity and Inclusion. Here are some issues I've come across that you should think about:

1. Don't assume that you understand someone's culture. You may have a shared experience, but it's not the same experience.

2. Don't assume that a woman isn't technical or interested in golf. "Oh, I didn't think to ask you, because I didn't think you cared."

3. You have a company library but not one book is from a diverse author. Obviously, you're not showing a commitment to Diversity and Inclusion.

4. You go to an outside meeting, and even though your staff isn't diverse, you say you're all one. No, we're not all one! That's nice in theory. Yes, we all want the same things – love, family, justice, etc. – but if diverse people appear only

EXPAND BEYOND YOUR CURRENT CULTURE

when you're speaking to someone who doesn't look like you, sound like you, and walk like you, then those diverse people are just props.

5. You ask staff what would make them feel more included and invested and then ignore what they say. So why did you ask?

6. Don't say, "Why do you celebrate that? We can't give you time off – use a personal day." It's not for you to ask why unless you really want to know more about it.

7. "You need a place to pray, pump, or pee?" Do I really need to explain why providing clean spaces for prayer and pumping are mandatory? As for peeing, gender neutral restrooms are an option. ADA-compliant restrooms on every floor are not optional. Gender neutral restrooms can be as easy as changing a sign and sending out a notice about the change. This will be appreciated as a first step. Here's what someone in the architecture, engineering, and construction (AEC) field said:

> Interesting to see the bias that exists around gender-neutral restrooms. We are designing more and more and having those conversations with clients.

8. "Geez, now we can't make jokes in the office if we're an inclusive office." If you were making jokes in your office that you need to think twice about, then that wasn't the correct place for

them anyway. Most likely nowhere was the correct place for them.

9. Are you hiding behind your title? You say, "You'd love to see changes, but there's just so much work to be done, and to stop and review company culture would be too much work. Is it really important? I'm very busy!" Yet your company says that it has a great company culture. Hmmmm . . .

10. You have diversity goals that are unrealistic. You have set goals and you're determined to make your numbers, so you hire and hire but don't ever seem to meet your goals. Have you made a retention goal along with a diversity goal?

11. Stop offering excuses for why you can't release your D&I numbers. We'll get into this a little later in the book. If you aren't committed to Diversity and Inclusion, stop talking about it! If you *are*, show your numbers!

Faking It Till They Make It

Below are some anonymous survey responses from a questionnaire I sent to people working in various fields (cited below each response) asking them how their companies have been faking it:

The horrible marketing ads that feature a woman of color and hiring a black woman who isn't empowered to make changes once in the position.

— *Meetings and Events*

The leadership within the organization talks about the importance of D&I and how we need to work on being more diverse and inclusive. However, no action has been implemented in this direction. Additionally, when offers arose about discussions about strategic planning to assist in rectifying this issue, they have been shot down.

— *Higher Education (University)*

The hiring of certain minority groups to make the company look inclusive, but the opinions, advisements, and upper executives do not match. The perception is all are welcome, but the reality is "keep your mouth shut."

— *Construction Risk Management and Insurance*

From my own experiences, they hired me for my skills and work ethic. But I think they just want to show they have a black person working for them. In reality, they don't really want you to be involved in decision-making that will help the company succeed.

— *Motion and Photography*

My company "fakes it till they make it" by using diverse populations as tokens rather than genuinely embracing the fact that both diverse internal audiences in the company significantly represent powerful knowledge, intelligence, and opportunity, while diverse external audiences represent incremental and growing spending power. Placing people of color on corporate brochures and internal documents, as if the current company environment is dedicated to supporting these communities, is very insulting and disrespectful to employees who exist in the day-to-day operations, which *are not* truly representative of the current company culture.

— Social Media/Marketing

Our church can't afford to fake it till we make it because our church must be a safe space for all.

— Faith Community

Our tagline is "Wellness For All." We believe in democratizing wellness regardless of class, race, or gender. We realize the limitations, as there is no way we can speak for all. But the best we can do is to hold space to embrace more inclusion, and to have the self-awareness to include more voices that are not our own.

— Wellness

Save the platitudes for an acceptance speech. Your actions are what matter.

— Media

Often companies commit to D&I because it looks good and sounds "progressive." However, often the internal messaging to the "D&I recruits" is "now you are in, stay in your lane!" That company recruits are referred to as D&I recruits in the first place is problematic.

— Event Executive

How does your company rate 1–10? Do you show the outside world all the good things you are doing but you haven't built a sustainable company culture and enough diversity? How do you get your insides and outsides to match?

— Biopharma Consultant

Advice for Leadership

I hope this chapter gives you an understanding that we see you, and if we work for you, we feel you. It's time to think differently! Believe it or not, the people who work for you want to help with the diversity of thought inside your company. When you present outside, they just don't want to be used as props.

What can you do today to make these changes in your company?

THINK
ABOUT
PEOPLE

CHAPTER 6

It's Time to Think Differently!

IT'S TIME TO THINK DIFFERENTLY about how we approach diversity, inclusion, and company culture:

People! We need to think about people!

When I was starting to write this book, I went to various bookstores in different states (yes, there are still brick and mortar bookstores). When I asked if they carried books on Diversity and Inclusion, I found that most stores had maybe two, and others said I could order them. When I said that I was writing a business book on Diversity and Inclusion, they looked at me as if I had two heads.

I was told that the books they had were in the race section, which was really the African American section. Before I could hold my tongue I said out loud, "Why the devil would a book on Diversity and Inclusion be in the race section? *We* know what the devil is going on! *We* know what it's like to be diverse! *We're* trying to get others to get it!"

At some bookstores they were in the Social Science section. Clearly, those books were written by PhDs. Nothing against PhDs – I have questions for them and look forward to working on the next book with them – but they take an academic approach to Diversity and Inclusion, and it's time to think differently!

At some stores I was told to speak with their book buyers, and they said, "Yeah, you're right, they should be in business as well as the other sections."

In the questionnaire that I talked about in the previous chapter I asked "What do you want leadership to know about Diversity and Inclusion?" (keep in mind that the people who filled out the questionnaire are from various industries, backgrounds, and ages). For some reason someone thought it was a great idea to use only data to make D&I decisions. They forgot to take into account that humans are on the other side of the data, and in order for data to work you need to know what humans are thinking and feeling (you also need diverse humans attached to researching the data). Here are some of the survey responses:

> I would let them know that their strategy needs to be authentic and rooted in cultural sensitivity. Long gone are the days of checking boxes – they need to understand that diversity needs to be thoughtful and purposeful, with a long-term plan.
>
> — *Education*

If I could speak to my current employer about Diversity and Inclusion, the first thing I would say is that they need to respect the importance of creating a consistent work environment and company culture in which *all* employees from different backgrounds, ethnicities, and sexual orientations feel welcome and respected. Rather than checking a box in the event of an internal or external audit by placing people of color only in corporate brochures and marketing materials when it's convenient for company optics, they must enforce an authentic and inclusive atmosphere on a regular basis, while demonstrating an unwavering commitment to diverse employees so they never feel they have to question if they're truly valued instead of being a PR/marketing tool.

From an external-facing perspective, I would suggest to my current employer that they continuously conduct consumer research so that marketing efforts are directed toward all audiences – e.g., adding more diverse representation on the company website because the depiction of who is using our products is not fully inclusive and only represents the Caucasian population. If given more time, research, and efforts, I'm sure it would be revealed that the people currently depicted on the company website are not fully representative of all audiences truly purchasing our products, i.e., African Americans, Hispanics, LGBTQ+ consumers.

— *Social Media/Marketing*

Succeeding in this world of constant change requires customer adaptability, which is a byproduct of having a culture of diversity in the workplace. Women play a leading role in 85 percent of auto purchasing decisions.

— *Auto Industry*

The organization should be welcoming to all, not just the worker who looks like a supermodel or the latest reality TV star. Everyone should be able to attend a client meeting in spite of their looks, race, or sexual orientation, and not just the workers who the organization feels comfortable with or the client won't have a problem with.

— *Construction*

If I could speak to my employer or anyone in leadership about Diversity and Inclusion, I would let them know that creating an inclusive workplace should not stop at just physical efforts like bringing on gender-neutral restrooms or making ramps for people who use wheelchairs. It should stretch to the workers' mindsets too. Some rules need to be set up to keep the "normal staff" well away from hurting the feelings of those who are either physically or emotionally different.

— *Entertainment/Writing*

It is imperative to think of the disabled community. . . . It should never be an afterthought. . . .

Clear cultural Diversity and Inclusion of persons with disabilities should be a part of all diversity training. It should be a part of the branding of every company. It's important to hire someone or train someone who has a clear understanding of ADA laws and requirements but also to not just do the bare minimum but truly embrace all they have to offer. It opens doors for your employee to know he/she has a bright future with a company that appreciates all they have to offer and not see them as an inconvenience.

— Travel & Disability

I suffer from mental illness – I can have some really emotional days like I had this week. I work in a good environment. . . . I can be open and honest and have tough conversations. I feel supported in growing my abilities and getting better. People want to see me succeed.

— Tech

As you can see it's time to look at how we treat those with disabilities in a new light. They are We & Us and not an add-on. The same goes for people of color.

Think Differently About . . .

Communication and Inclusion

Let's break down what it means when we say the words *diversity, equity, inclusion,* and *company culture.*

When we use these terms we need to make sure that we're all clear about their meanings so we're all on the same page. Communication is half the battle. We shouldn't assume that we know what someone means when they use these words. For example, *inclusion* to you may mean just having folks who don't look like you in the room. *Inclusion* to others and to me means not only *being* in the room but also *being welcomed* in the room with the same access as others in the room.

Diversity

Diversity may mean that your company has employees who don't walk like you, look like you, or sound like you. Diversity for many is skin tone, love interest, and/or disabilities you can see. But that doesn't always include diversity of thought.

Diversity of thought and diversity of thinking are two different things. One is people who bring creative ideas that complement yours. The other is people who think differently. Do you want one of them in your company? Both?

You need to think about how you diversify your program offerings, your leadership, your offices, your warehouse, your product offerings. Diversity goes beyond gender and race. It's also about thought – how you see things and how you implement them. Diversity means that you accept me and don't see me as a threat to you or your thoughts. Our different ways of thinking can be useful when we reach across borders to customers. Diversity means that we get to share our cultures and thinking with each other.

Diversity gives your company an edge in any marketplace and raises its bottom line. Not only does the company have a variety of talent, it has an in-house focus group to tweak ideas before sending them outside the company. Diversity helps you win!

Company Culture

Think about how you build your company culture so that it matches the mission of your business and works for your values.

Equity

Equity is allowing people to be deeply invested in their projects and letting them contribute their knowledge to other projects. Equity means that people know when opportunities arise, not after the fact but before the fact, and that they have the opportunity to pitch for them. Equity means that they get a raise based on their merit, not on their gender or race. People don't want equal, they want what's theirs.

Disability

When you speak of disabilities, do you mean only the ones you can see? Do you ever consider those who have disabilities that you can't see? What are your policies around wellness? Or does wellness mean yoga to you?

Age

Do you look at someone of a certain age and say that they're no longer part of your company culture? Or, do you say that they're a fountain of information? Do you use them to the best of their abilities? How many times have you said that they look good for their age? How many times have you said that you can't believe they're still working at their age?

Personal Attributes

What do you think of those who may not fit the body image of the company culture? Is the way they look more important than their talent? Do you hide them away and exhibit only those who fit the image you want? Or are you thinking differently?

Agencies

Are you thinking differently about the agencies you work with? Is their work successful? Do they understand not only your project goals but your company goals? I ask this because recently there was a backlash about a project concerned with changing the covers of classic books and redoing bookstore displays for Black History Month. The project assumed that you could just slap a black face on the cover of books written about white people by white authors and, presto, they're diverse. Many agencies worked on this project, and clearly they weren't the right ones. The agencies may be good, but they weren't good for this project. How many of the people who signed off on the project celebrate Black History Month and thought this was a good idea? Figure out what you're trying to achieve, and if you want to be diverse and inclusive you need to be able to share what that means to you and to those who aren't you.

If you don't know, ask. It's time to stop thinking you're the only smart one in the room. It's time to reach out and listen to what's being said to you and to take advice even when it makes you uncomfortable. It's time to practice active listening. It's time to think differently and to realize that understanding and respecting a culture aren't the same as being born in it.

Story Time

I owned a company that produced branded and luxury events. I had two very different experiences when I was hired by Asian market executives who produced events for the Asian-American market. Kudos to them for seeing the talent I could bring to the events and not the color of my skin. Thanks to Grace Lee, Joe Lam and others!

My First Experience: Asian Branded Events

I was called into the office to have the first big idea meeting, and as I walked into the conference room, one of the Asian brand managers looked at me and said, "Why are you here? I didn't think this was for the urban market. Why is the urban agency here?"

Those of you who don't know me can't imagine the face I gave him as I stated, "Number one, I'm not an urban agency. I happen to be black and I'll stay black, but I'm responsible for the Asian roll-out. Do you have an issue?" Before he could answer, the head of that division came in and immediately said to everyone, "If you don't know Leslie, her agency (K.I.M. Media) will be handling all branded events for this launch." The take-away is that it was the Asian brand manager's problem that he thought a black woman couldn't handle a luxury launch in the Asian market.

My Second Experience: Asian Culture

I handled many events for the Asian market, and working with some of the Asian agencies was challenging because it's part of their culture that they don't like to say no, but I would say no when it needed to be said. They finally realized that, and the owner of the agency called and said that I was strict, but I respected their culture and he wanted me on his team.

I will always praise that owner for seeing beyond our differences in working styles, that we were better together, and that I did respect his culture. I understood because I had lived in Asia for over three years and owned a business there. I understood the sensibilities but never assumed that I knew everything. He went outside his culture and the norm of how he did business and brought in someone who thought differently to enhance the big picture.

FUBU The Collection

Here's one last story on thinking differently (I have so many) so that you understand that it's not only about color. When I was offered the job at FUBU The Collection I made it very clear that I didn't know about hip hop, that it wasn't my world. I traveled the world and lived in Europe for over ten years and in Japan for over three; for the last year-and-a-half I owned a business there. When I returned to the states most of my friends were from my European and Asian days, and my new friends were in the arts, entertainment, and advertising world, but not in the hip hop world.

When I told the CEO that I didn't know anything about hip hop, he said that I didn't need to, that he had those contacts and would share them with me. He said that he needed me to bring CNN and other outlets from my world on board, and that would be how we would grow. I was with the company for ten years as President of Marketing, Advertising & PR.

He thought differently. It would have been easy for him to say that they needed to solidify their market before expanding, so they would rather have someone who knew their current market. Years later he would say that I may not have grown up like him, but I got it, I understood the market, domestic and international, and I could speak to everyone (although sometimes a little too fast). He said that having someone with vastly different life experiences would be beneficial in the long run.

———

If diversity, inclusion, and an authentic company culture are supposed to be part of your foundation, then you'll need to think outside yourself, stop counting numbers, and start looking at people and what they can offer. People don't use all of their skills every day, but if they're given the opportunity for growth, you'll be surprised what skills will shine when they're needed.

I saw a posting from a speaker who invited people to hear her speak about diversity and her commitment to it. She said it would be fun. Instead of calling it fun,

I thought she should invite people to enjoy an informative evening of lively conversation on how we're all committing to Diversity and Inclusion. *Fun* makes me think that people aren't serious about the conversation, that it's just a night out on the town, but *informative* leads me to think I'll learn something new. It's time to learn something new from the old conversations we've been having. It's time to execute with thoughtfulness, research, and a strong cultural team.

It's time for all of us to think differently. If you're a black person or a person of color and want things to be different, you have to stand up and say so. And if your friends are thinking differently, then, in the words of Rihanna, "Tell your friends to pull up." I know black folks and people of color are tired of feeling like we need to teach everyone about our culture. Well, we do, so we need to think differently about being tired, because I'd rather teach folks what I'll accept than have them assume they know.

Here's one more example of why we need to be teachers:

> At my former firm, I attended a meeting at a client's headquarters. During a coffee break the client's senior R&D executive, a man in his early 40s, said (having seen me in the room), "Sometimes I wish I were a woman of color. I could get whatever job I want with none of the qualifications, a signing bonus, and a holy guarantee that I'll never get fired."
>
> — *Biopharma Consultant*

It's Time for All of Us to Think Differently!

Us

Us

Us

Us

Us

Us

Us

Us

Us

Us

Us

Us

Us

Us

Us

AVOID
SILOS

CHAPTER 7

Diversity and Inclusion Should Not Be Built in Silos

THE VERY COMMITTEES set up to develop a more inclusive company culture often cause segregation – segregation inclusion. Sometimes these committees and cultural groups cause more problems than they solve. You have African American, Asian, Hispanic, LGBTQ+, and women's groups. I haven't heard of a disabilities group (it may be called a wellness group).

Great! Now you have the groups, and some are well attended. Now what? Does a designated person attend all the meetings, hear the issues, and take them back to the D&I main committee and leadership? Do they then address the issues the best they can? Do you form groups because you've checked the boxes, and when it's their month or holiday (Black History, Lunar New Year) do you expect events from them? Do you then send an email to everyone in the company saying, "Event in conference room 2," and then ignore them until the next year?"

I would think that the head of D&I would have the ability to ensure that the groups and committees have

83

a purpose. Part of the purpose would be to ensure that those who are diverse feel included even when they're not sitting in the diversity group setting. If the groups themselves have issues, then someone has to unpack what's happening in them and, if necessary, take the issues to leadership.

If you build these groups, it's your duty to ensure that they're not trying to figure things out on their own and that any results are communicated to the rest of the company. You don't want the outcome of these groups to be that everyone thinks that the whole Diversity and Inclusion thing isn't working because people are still complaining. If they're complaining it's because all you've done is put a group of people together whose work isn't part of the foundation of the company.

I'm an advocate for a great organization that does an amazing job building diverse groups that are invested in their mission. The problem that most organizations face is that these groups are often kept away from each other. Companies take the time to build diversity in pockets, but they don't fold that diversity into the larger organization. You shouldn't just pluck and pull only what's beneficial to your specific cause. When people feel that the diversity is one-sided, you'll lose them.

Thoughts About Committees and Groups

In my questionnaire, I asked for people's thoughts about D&I committees and groups. Here are some of the responses:

In general, it's one thing to create a committee or D&I group to just have to fit in with the status quo. It's another thing to invest in the proper manpower and resources to get the job done.

— Education & Communications

This is my first workplace to have them. I appreciate it a lot. I never knew that it existed!

— Tech

My experience with groups has been that they're ill-trained and lacking true substance. They were created mostly to meet a requirement or to adhere to prior litigation.

— Travel & Disability, Executive Development

I think committees and groups are a good first step, but like anything else they need to be sustainable and collaborative to grow. You can't expect a one-sided monologue to lead to a conversation. The definition of conversation is a talk between two people or two sides.

— Entertainment & Tech

I think there are benefits and risks. The benefits are employee buy-in and execution – when people are a part of the process, they have a sense of ownership all the way through. The risk is that the right people aren't in the room and a qualified leader isn't there to keep them on task and accountable.

— Education

It's great to have a voice, but they may want to give consideration to how that voice is used. The very existence of a D&I committee, if they're not careful, can be an advertisement to everyone that diverse individuals are thought of as lesser and in need of special assistance. For the diverse individual, it can feel daunting.

— Financial Services

I think it's a fantastic, innovative idea. It shows that the company cares.

— Garment Industry

HR departments should all have special-needs sections to address disabilities and diversity.

— Medical

Everyone should be included and educated.

— Meetings & Events

Having these types of groups keeps leadership and the organization accountable in addition to being able to contribute to the growth and development of an organization by providing their insight.

— Higher Education (University)

They are only impactful and successful when they allow people to be vulnerable and, when necessary, uncomfortable. Contrary to popular belief, D&I groups aren't there to make us feel good, they're supposed to teach us how to accept and work through those uncomfortable feelings and thoughts that arise when we confront our own biases.

— *Technology*

As you've read, groups can be amazing as long as they have substance and purpose and their information is shared throughout the company and not kept inside the group. When you create groups, be prepared to hear real feedback on what's working and what isn't.

I've noticed that when a company gets into trouble they immediately say that they'll give money and set up an internal committee and groups to deal with the trouble. But part of the reason they got into trouble is that their staff isn't diverse and they don't have diversity of thought, so who's going to be a part of these groups and committees? And after they build them, what will they do with the information they collect? If the company had been serious about Diversity and Inclusion, that information would have informed their decisions and they wouldn't be in trouble in the first place.

You can't build it and expect Them to come! Make sure that the people you would like to benefit from the committees are building them.

I found in my research that the few people who were happy about the committees had seen change, big or small, in their companies. They had seen that thoughts and feelings were being shared between groups throughout the company. Purposeful committees aren't built in silos.

Inclusion and Groups

Inclusion is not only about belonging. Stop calling inclusion belonging – they have different meanings. It doesn't mean that everyone likes you; it means that you feel welcome in your space with others. Sometimes groups can make you feel even less wanted than you did before they were formed. They can make you feel like you've been asked to sit in a corner and not speak until spoken to, and even then you must give the right answer in order to be heard.

Make sure that whoever is creating the groups and committees for you is a good listener and communicator. That person needs to capture and incorporate information as needed for the benefit of those in the groups or committees and for the growth of the company.

A final thought on inclusion in silos. Keep in mind that there are 365 days a year. I'd appreciate it, as I'm sure others would, if you didn't call me to speak just during Black History Month. I have things to offer the other eleven months as well. I will continue to be black the other eleven months, and my message is needed the other eleven months.

When I was responsible for several celebrity clothing lines, and I handled their press and advertising, several fashion editors would call me when it was time for the "Urban" fashion layout or during Black History Month. I would ask, "Why are you calling me now. I reached out to you in the past and got no response." Of course, they would say, "We need black designers for *this* issue." You can guess my response: "What happened to the other issues? Thanks, but no thanks." I was always very clear with editors that they needed to treat my clients like any other fashion designers.

This is an example of segregation inclusion. We'll invite you in, but only when we need you.

The *New York Times* published an article about whether a white guy would wear clothing that retailers called "urban hip-hop streetwear." (I called it what it was – young men's clothing.) I wrote to them asking when clothing had become a color issue.

We're quick to put people and items in silos and then say, hey, we made this group or event or advertising just for you. But if it's not connected to the larger picture, focus, mission, foundation, then it has very little meaning. Again, thanks but no thanks.

The next time you approve a group, ask yourself how it connects to the rest of the company. Ask yourself who will be sharing thoughts that can assure the growth of not only the group but the company as a whole.

Inclusion Fatigue

I hear that some folks are having inclusion fatigue. We sure know how to get out of doing something by tacking a name on it and pushing it aside! If you've caught inclusion fatigue, better rest up, because you're going to be fatigued for some time to come!

When will that time be over? When you and others aren't using bias, racism, homophobia, ableism, anti-Semitism, sizeism, ageism, religious intolerance, xenophobia, classism, and all the other prejudices as an excuse to make people feel that they're not included.

—

**Inclusion is not a problem to solve
but an opportunity to seize.**

—

MAKE SURE THAT THE PEOPLE IN THE ROOM **LOOK LIKE THE PEOPLE** YOU'RE TRYING TO *REACH*

CHAPTER 8

Nothing About Us Without Us!

Tʜᴇʏ & Tʜᴇᴍ. When's it gonna be We & Us? It's gonna be We & Us when you stop making the same mistakes over and over and over!

Nothing About Us Without Us has many meanings to me. Let's start with the first one, which should be obvious, but judging by the news stories I've seen lately it clearly isn't.

You Need the Right People in the Room

For all that is right and righteous, if you're creating a program, shooting an ad campaign, or doing a role-play, and everyone in the room looks like you and sounds like you, then you're already headed down a black hole. I'm not saying that you need to include people of all cultures, ages, weights, etc., but you need to have people in the room with the same life experience as the people you're trying to reach. No exceptions, no excuses!

Here's another way of saying it. If you're doing a role-playing exercise, and everyone in the room looks like you, then you're really doing a high school play, not a role-play. A role-play gives you feedback on feelings. Until you have lived, not walked, but lived, in someone else's shoes, you may have an understanding, but you cannot have the same feelings.

If you're speaking about or planning something regarding someone who isn't like you, then you need to consult with appropriate cultural groups to get a better understanding of the people you're trying to deal with!

If you have a D&I officer, bring them into the meetings when issues are being worked on; don't wait until things have been decided. If you've hired that person to run your D&I department, make sure that they're in every meeting where you're working on new products, policy, programs, packaging, and cultural outreach. They also need the power to pull in others. They should be part of your C-suite team!

If I'm working on something about the LGBTQ+ community, you better believe I'm calling plenty of friends and friends of friends in that community to ask questions. Take a moment to think before you leap into a project, because it's clear whether you've made the effort or not made the effort to research and respect a culture. Just because you've seen it or done it in the past doesn't mean that it's right for this moment. If you don't know, ask! (Maybe that should have been the title of this book!)

When you're starting a project, you need inclusion of thought as well as cultural inclusion. Having a personal relationship with someone from a culture that's not yours may give you insight into that culture, but it doesn't make you an expert. It's not the same as being on the inside.

You can hold internal focus groups, but only if your staff is diverse. (It's sort of a Catch-22 – if you don't have diversity in your company you can't have an effective internal focus group on diversity.) One option is to hire a company to conduct a focus group for you, but you'll need to give them the proper information to conduct an effective focus group that will give you the insights you need for your project. This means that you'll need a focus group for the focus group. Another option is to hire consultants who can help you reach out to the diverse groups you're trying to reach out to. For example, if you're trying to speak to black folks during an election, there are educated black folks and points of contact outside the church. Just saying.

I hope that I've made my meaning clear. If not, call me. We'll go for coffee or a drink and I'll be happy to break it down further.

Avoid Mixed Messages

What's happening internally in your company? Does Public Relations know what Advertising is doing? Does Advertising know what Marketing is doing? Does Social Media and Sales have the concept and context of the goal of the mission and campaign? This is where I see things go awry. I've read your press release. I've seen your ad. I've seen your post. I've seen your products in stores.

But it's obvious that somewhere a breakdown in communications happened! Why? Because you are clearly sending mixed messages! And now you're in a mess!

Communication is the key. How is your message being said? Who's saying it? Where is it being said? Who's in the ad? Just because it's a celebrity and you think it's cool doesn't mean that he can be dressed as an Indian chief. It's not cool – it's a mess if you haven't researched your market or if all your departments aren't on the same page. What-A-Mess!

Someone on the inside should have pointed the mess out to you. PR, Marketing, Advertising, Staff? If you don't have diversity of thought you won't understand cultural references and meanings. Now you're in trouble!

Story Time

See the Pattern?

I love stories. When I came back to America I modeled as my side gig, and I landed a large national campaign. Having lived out of the country for thirteen years I was in the habit of asking about hair and make-up. I always brought wigs and makeup with me because more times than not the people running the campaign weren't prepared, even though they told me not to worry. If *I* hadn't been prepared, I would have been sorry.

> *Client:* We would like to test adding extensions to your hair.

> *Me:* Does the hair stylist know how to work with black hair?

NOTHING ABOUT US WITHOUT US!

Client: Yes, he does tons of 7th on Sixth Shows (New York Fashion Week).

Me: Hmm, OK.

Client: We'll do a test for styles.

Me: Great, I'll be there.

[Arrive at client office with their staff, hairstylist, and several executives present.]

Hairstylist: I'll add a few extensions just to mock the styles for this evening.

Me: That's great. Please keep in mind my agent mentioned that I'm booked for a job tomorrow, so please make sure that whatever we do tonight can come out and that we're not gluing.

Hairstylist: I have glue that will rub out.

Me: You do see I'm black, right, and with black hair nothing rubs out, and we're in the office and not a salon.

Long story short, the hairstylist didn't work on the final campaign because the glue *didn't* rub out. I had to be paid to have my hair redone and for the job that had to be pushed back (fortunately they switched me with another model at the last minute so I could have an extra day to find a stylist who could help), all at the cost of the client.

I should have spoken up sooner, but, like many people, I didn't want to cause trouble. and yet we often end up in worse trouble when we keep quiet. I will never hold back again. Remember, if you want to cross over into other cultures, hire people who can do the job and listen to them!

The moral of this story also applies to women and those with disabilities and LGBTQ+ folks and so on. I don't want you to think that this is just a color issue. Stop assuming that you know it all about the people you're trying to reach. Bring those educated about the topic into the room and together you can make informed decisions.

You might be thinking that Diversity and Inclusion requires a lot of time and money, and you're right. You may have to add a line item called research to your budget, unless you want to add a line item called additional legal fees.

I speak from experience. It was my job. I've been They & Them in the room, and I've been the consultant hired to be in the room to insure that They & Them in the room had a voice. If you call us into the room, don't do it for show, do it because you're invested in getting it right.

Advice for Leadership

I asked the following question in my questionnaire: If you could tell leadership anything about *Nothing About Us Without Us*, what would it be?

Include Us in the conversation.

— *Promotion, Marketing & Event Planning*

No policy should be decided by any representative without the participation of members of the group affected by that policy.

— *Auto Industry*

Leadership should know that ideas, especially those on a massive level, should be heard by a diverse group in order to ensure sensitivity and improve overall appeal.

— *Media*

As a member of the Latinx community, I have to say that no one person can make the decision for the entire community, since we are really a multi-colored, multi-cultured, multi-dialect group. We need to be consulted as individuals before implementing anything that may affect us.

— *Garment Industry*

Do not ignore or be oblivious to the need to take a comprehensive approach when making changes. Being proactive in taking the necessary steps to foster full representation and participation of all groups being impacted by the changes considered is what needs to be accomplished.

— *Higher Education (University)*

Equal pay should be for all races, genders, and the genderless.

— *Construction Risk Management/Insurance*

I want them to listen to us because we know our culture and we need to be part of any decision when it comes to our culture.

— *Motion & Photography*

Include a diverse selection of voices in decisions that affect the company policies, culture, benefits, and strategic plan.

— *Education*

They should get involved and get their hands dirty at the grassroots level, not just sit in their ivory tower and make decisions without even being physically present among their staff. Regular forums should be held, even on a one-on-one basis (since many staff would be uncomfortable being completely honest in a group setting), on what staff like and don't like, what would cause them to leave or to stay, etc. People need to have candid conversations with no fear of judgment or of losing their job.

— *Financial Services*

Artificial Intelligence

Before we move on to the next chapter, I would be remiss if I didn't discuss artificial intelligence (AI) and algorithms. I'm a true believer in tech and that it can be used for good. It can also be used to oppress those who don't understand it and have a hard time using it.

AI is used for hiring. The "experts" speak about it as if it's magical, like the Wizard of Oz. But if you pull back the curtain, you'll see there's a person program-ming the mysterious black box of AI, and what's pro-grammed in determines what the algorithms give back. So, if white men are giving other white men directions for hiring, and that's what's programmed into the box, where's the diversity?

You've probably heard of the studies on AI hiring. You take two copies of the same resume, and you put an ethnic-sounding name on one copy and a non-ethnic-sounding name on the other. One resume gets tagged for an interview, the other doesn't. Guess which one gets tagged.

If you're going to use algorithms as part of your hir-ing process you need to have diverse people on the com-mittee that decides what qualifications you're looking for (*Nothing About Us Without Us!*). If you're not involv-ing diverse people in your process, you can't just shrug and blame the AI – "Hey, the machine gave us what the machine gave us." Non-diverse input means non-diverse output. Garbage in, garbage out. No excuses!

Moving On

There are no excuses for not including diversity of thought in your decision-making, and anyone in the room who doesn't speak up is responsible for that lack of diversity.

Here are some important questions to ask yourself for your cultural check-up:

1. Have we expanded beyond our current culture to get additional opinions as we develop the project, policy, whatever?

2. Do we have the right people in the room to help us make decisions that will benefit the majority? (You can't please everyone.)

3. Have we researched the culture we're trying to reach? (This includes your company culture.)

4. Have we brought in others to review the project before releasing it, just in case our research is off?

5. What's the meaning behind this outreach?

6. Have we done all we can do to make this successful?

7. Have we had everyone at the table? Head of D&I, Public Relations, Advertising, Marketing, Social Media, Consultants?

8. Does everyone understand the What, How, and Why?

9. Is Human Resources up to date on what to ask for from algorithms? Do they know how to direct the companies being asked to handle the search before it reaches HR?

10. Is this a true representation of my company and the message we're trying to share?

11. Have I moved beyond reporting the numbers?

12. Has this been reviewed as a Zero Risk bias?

_____

Remember, it takes a shorter time to ask the right questions than it does to recover from a misstep.

_____

_____

If you are using the lack of diversity and culture to get press

– we see you.

_____

Nothing About Us Without Us!

If you take only one thing from this book, this is it. This is the phrase you should think of any time you create policy, procedures, programing, advertising, public relations, hiring, writing, and outreach.

Who is in the room with you? Do they look like the people you're trying to reach?

IF YOU AREN'T
COMMITTED
TO THE WORK,

DON'T SAY
YOU ARE
DOING THE
WORK

CHAPTER 9

Be Committed to the Work

Trending hashtags: #diversityandinclusion #inclusion #companyculture #culture #race #gender #disabilities #leadership #diversity #lgbtq #equality #cultural diversity

———

FOLKS ARE QUICK TO ADD HASHTAGS to their company post. They use the words *diversity* or *diverse*. They speak about how their company mission is inclusive, how inclusion is part of their company culture, and how they won't discriminate because of race, gender, or disabilities.

They say that leadership and advancement are important to them and that this sets the tone of the company – blah, blah, blah . . .

For the companies that are honestly doing the work, Bravo! The sad part is that most companies love to *talk* about the work, but they don't *do* the work needed to create a diverse and inclusive company culture. It sounds great when it's in a press release, tweet, or post, but for those working with you it's an empty promise.

Stop acting like you care if you don't! It's time for action. It's hard, but it's not that hard. Some companies want to take the easy way out by sponsoring a party, an event, a scholarship. Those things are great, and you should continue to do them, but they're not enough. You can check a box or two, but it's not really doing the needed work.

I've been asked to do full assessments of leadership, space, and staff for companies. I love this work because I get to sit down with leadership and explain my process and hear what else they've thought about since engaging me to work with them. We agree on direction, but after I've done the assessments, when I tell them my findings, I often get blank stares. Sometimes they say they don't believe that their staff actually said what I've reported. I tell them again how the information was gathered, and advise them on the areas of concern that need to be addressed and the direction they should take.

When they get over their surprise at hearing some of the staff comments they begin to focus and I tell them that now the real work begins. Some CEOs roll up their sleeves raring to make changes! They realize that it's not going to be easy, but they're all in. Others fight me with excuses on timing, budget, and feelings. (What's in their bags?) I tell them that it's time to make change happen. Without change they're just making empty promises, making everything worse for them.

Action Is Required

Diversity and Inclusion is not a trend! The words are trending, but there needs to be more action, much more. You can add these words and all the ones I hashtagged at the top of the chapter into all your company branding, handbooks, and advertising, but if you aren't making a real effort to insure that you have a diverse company, you're just faking it. No one wants to work in a place that doesn't believe in its own mission.

Here are some excuses that I've heard, and others that have been shared with me, when I call out a company and ask them to stop talking about the work and do it.

- "We do the best we can . . ." – Honestly? Your best? Do you need help being better?

- "It takes time to get everyone on board to make change . . ." – Agreed. So let's start now.

- "We believe we are diverse . . ." – What does diverse mean to you? Let's build from there.

- "We do something for Women's Month, Black History Month . . ." – Not enough!

- "Budgets . . ." – What do budgets have to do with assuring that your company does what it says it does?

They understand that it's important, but there's not enough emphasis put on it.

— *Architecture, Engineering, and Construction*

Doing the work means that staff and leadership communicate with each other to assure that the company continues to review its programming so that it's relevant to the times and to its mission.

Maybe you've supported a program or sponsorship, or had someone of a different culture working for you in the past, but that's just the past. What have you done lately? If you're not doing it today or, as someone said, "creating impactful actions tied to intention," then it's time for you to stop pretending that you care.

As I said earlier, if you don't plan on hiring a head of D&I then stop advertising for one. You may think that it makes you look good to advertise, but when the ad runs for months and there's still no head of D&I, it's obvious to everyone that you're not serious. You can tell everyone you're making the effort, but everyone knows you're just checking one of your boxes.

Board Members

Let's touch on your board. You claim that your company is diverse, but your board isn't. You keep saying that you're looking to diversify your board. You talk about adding a woman. (Notice the "a.") A white woman? Is the face of your diversity a white woman? Does that qualify you to stop doing anything else?

Seek out board members who have a diversity of thought, whose resources and understanding of your industry can add value. Added value is for the company, not only for the press release.

Pledges

You go to conferences and take tons of notes as black folks and people of color speak, then you go back to your office and do nothing! Or you get excited about implementing something you've heard, but then you make excuses for why it can't happen at this time. If it can't happen now, just say so. Or say nothing. No need to call me to tell me why it can't happen.

Commitment

What does it mean to commit to the work?

I moderated a conference panel and asked this very question. What does commitment look like and feel like? Here are some of the responses:

- Equity equals access
- Inclusion
- Compatible market salaries
- Representation on all levels in the company
- Representation in the agencies you work with
- Community engagement throughout the year
- Cultural awareness and understanding
- Continued education for leadership, staff, and board
- Diversity of thinking
- Asking cultural questions when making decisions that affect others

- Speaking about the things that may not be working and why
- Not checking the boxes
- A D&I statement that you live up to and not just post

Employees understand the values, beliefs, and organizational mission that get reiterated daily through word and action.

— Higher Education (University)

————

Your customers will notice if you focus on your commitment. It will be beneficial to your bottom line, your employees, your board, and your bragging rights!

————

TO SEE A RETURN YOU MUST INVEST FIRST

CULTURE
IS NOT SOMETHING YOU
SPEAK ABOUT

IT'S SOMETHING YOU
CREATE

CHAPTER 10

Create an Authentic Company Culture

CULTURE ISN'T SOMETHING YOU SPEAK ABOUT, it's something you create. And it takes more than a pool table and some beer to create an authentic company culture. Authentic cultures are made by understanding and trying to include the views of everyone in the company.

When I ask people to describe their company culture, I normally get two answers: "We have none" or "We get free stuff . . ." So then I ask, "How does it feel going to work each day? You get free stuff, so things are great, right?" That's when people's faces change. One woman said, "The free stuff is nice. I'm not a woman who would turn down a wine-and-cupcake day. But if you think that if the company gives me free things that I won't notice that my voice isn't valued, that I see leadership has little direction, and that we're working in circles, then think again. The company has failed to create an authentic company culture."

I consulted with a company where the woman I spoke to told me that her company was cool, that they just had a bit of an inclusion issue.

Needless to say, she was surprised when I said that her company culture was not cool because lack of inclusion is one of the main reasons that people leave their jobs. I then asked when they had last had a department meeting on company culture. Or a leadership meeting on company culture. Needless to say, I wasn't surprised when she said they hadn't had *any*.

I spoke to a company that focuses on companies' financial portfolios, and I was told that Diversity and Inclusion is too hard to quantify, that tangible metrics are needed to understand the company's financial position.

But there *are* companies that collect data on Diversity and Inclusion. Hiding behind the "lack of data" is just one more excuse you give to those who work for you and to those who buy your products or use your services for not doing what's right. Keep in mind that once the data is collected you need to use the data to make changes.

I know how business works, and I know for a fact that whether people are black, brown, white, or red, or purple people eaters, if they come in your door with green (or plastic), they're your kind of people. If you don't respect them, and by respect I mean treat them fairly, their green is going to go elsewhere! People don't want to spend money with companies that don't treat them, and by extension their own employees, decently.

Company Culture Is Either Painful or Pleasurable

Painful

When people are unhappy with management, whether it's lack of direction, low salaries, or personalities, what's the first thing they do? You know the answer – they tell anyone who will listen how unhappy they are. Day in and day out they'll complain and try to get others on their side. This slows down work and wears down other employees, and, God forbid, they take their unhappiness to social media.

There are companies today that wish that all they had to deal with was social media and not the lawsuits aimed at hostile working environments and bad company culture.

Pleasurable

People are happy at work when their company culture encourages the following:

1. A human capital focus

2. Creating community – promoting a team approach rather than an individual approach to work

3. Valuing ideas, input, feedback, and support from members all across the organization and at any level

4. Integrating age, race, and gender so that everyone is equal in conversations

5. Leadership who are engaged with the whole staff

6. Communication – letting people know what's happening whether it's good or bad

7. An emphasis on individual success and how that helps everyone else

8. True implementation of anti-harassment laws and codes of conduct

9. Respecting what individuals bring of themselves to the job

10. Diversity of culture

11. Diversity of thinking

12. Understanding that people of other cultures can find some jokes and body language insulting, and expecting people to stand up when they see it or hear it

13. Knowing that inside the company there are allies, champions, and advocates

14. Commitment to do the work inside and outside the company

The Most Important Aspects of Company Culture

I want to emphasize the following three aspects of company culture because they're so important. (These were shared by a professional in a lobbying and public relations firm).

Respect

I think one of the most powerful ways to show respect in an office is to make sure that every team member has knowledge of their role. This includes everyone from the CEO to the secretary. When we know what others do, it allows us to interact with one another in a respectful manner, creating a "we couldn't do it without you and we're all in this together" attitude.

Respect for each individual and what they bring to the table and how it can be used at the table.

Solution-based Thinking

I've worked so many times with and for people who are great at pointing out the problems, but never offer solutions. It causes a really negative environment at work and makes folks less likely to want to work together. Leave Negative Nancy in the lobby and bring in some optimism. Allowing coworkers to feel like they're walking into a discussion about solutions also helps diverse opinions find their way into the discussion.

Self-awareness

You're the CEO. You may have vision, but that doesn't mean you have a grasp of every way possible to make it happen. Surrounding yourself with only people who look and think like you is a disservice to you and the company. Diversity in your staff will mean a further-reaching network and more opportunity to grow in every direction.

Story Time

When was the last time you reviewed your company mission statement, vision statement, and company handbook? These documents are your foundation, and as with any foundation they need to be examined regularly for cracks, stains, and decay.

There was a story in the news about an ex-employee who came back to his company after five years and killed some of the employees and himself. We've heard other stories like this, and often the problems started with how the ex-employees were treated while they worked at their company. In the story I mentioned, the employee found a noose at his locker and reported it, and not much was done about it. In another incident, a university student was told to wear a racist and culturally insensitive prop for a fashion show. When the student said that she was uncomfortable with props that depicted black stereotypes, she was told that it was only for a short time and to get on with it.

How you respond to your employees, and the outside world, in situations like these will affect how your current employees see your commitment to diversity, inclusion, and an authentic company culture.

———

Here's a very different outcome from a company that supports Diversity and Inclusion. To date I've only heard positive stories from its employees.

This company promoted an African American-owned business, a new vendor in the store, with a national commercial. (This kind of thing wasn't new for this company – they had already been advertising a full spectrum of diverse people.) The ad featured the owner of the business, who is black and a woman, who said that she was proud to show black girls what they could achieve.

That one statement started an avalanche of white women asking how she dared to leave out white girls. It was twisted from being a cultural empowerment statement to being a race statement. But in spite of the discord, sales went up. African Americans bought her products and supported her and asked why shouldn't they speak about representation. After all, black vendors don't get a lot of support in major stores.

This is a story of company culture because this company stood by their mission of serving and supporting diverse communities at all levels of their company. The company, by the way, was Target. If I worked there, I would stand a little taller knowing that the company I work for sees me. I'm not saying they're perfect I'm saying Bravo Target for your Diversity and Inclusion efforts. I see you!

Cultural Culture

I'm an activist for several organizations, and recently I was on a panel to discuss how we could advance our cultures together. My other panelists were open and honest, and the audience asked honest questions. A few things came up that I'd like to share because, as I've said before, inclusion and culture go beyond the board-room or the office, they're about who you are before you enter the workplace.

How do we advance our cultures together? For starters, it can't be a one-way street. Don't call me only when you need me – that is, when you need a woman, or a black woman, or an extra body, or to show that you have friends from other cultures.

It's about what I call *cultural culture*. I told the audi-ence, "I will stand with you when you need me, I will stand with you when you're not present, I will stand with you with the knowledge you share with me, and I will share it with others. Will you stand with me when I step off the stage and you see me on the street or in the hotel lobby?"

I watched the blood drain from some of the faces in the audience. I said that if we want to share cultures and want to include cultures, it's not enough to just talk about it. We must lead by example. We must show oth-ers that we walk together because it's right and not just because we want something in return. We must learn from and respect each other for what we share with each other.

How can we learn about other cultures, and what can we do?

Ask questions if you don't understand. Talk about your own culture, and if it's near a cultural holiday explain the meaning of the holiday and how you cel-ebrate. (If you're comfortable doing it, invite others to share in the holiday with you.) Reach outside your neighborhood and take your family to eat at a restaurant of a different culture. Volunteer, not as a savior but to learn and to share what you've learned. Visit a church, temple, or mosque. Be a good visitor – respect the traditions as you would want yours to be respected.

When you get to work, hold on to the feeling you had when you visited these different places, the feeling of being the one, the only one, who was different. Then think about your employees and how you can build a company culture that respects their differences so that they want to work with you and not against you. You must recognize that a white woman and a black woman in the same position, getting the same pay, in the same company, will still be different.

The privilege that comes with not having to think about whether someone fits in is the very privilege that blocks you from growing as a person and as a company.

Company Culture and Your Workspace

Company culture is also about how your office looks, feels, and smells. If you work in a mess it will wear on your spirit, and if you work in the most futuristic office and it has no life, no feeling, and no energy, then it's up to you as leaders to make it come to life.

I consulted with a company that hosted an executive workshare space. I could have told the companies that rented from us, here are the amenities, go to it. But I knew that those CEOs or company owners wanted a space they would be comfortable in, where they could entertain clients with pride, as well as enjoy the benefits we offered. So, I made sure that my staff and I were always available to chat or whatever. I created a space where individuals cared about what the others in that space were doing even though they weren't involved in those businesses. That's an authentic company culture.

My friends who work remotely have begged me to write about how disconnected they feel from their companies. They feel like stepchildren, doing the work but not being a part of things. They're sometimes left out of meetings, birthdays, and other invites. (It's nice to be invited even if you can't make it.)

How do you include employees when they work remotely? Videoconference whenever you can. Make sure that those employees receive notices of birthdays, celebrations, and updates. The whole team and leadership should check in weekly. If remote workers are working from a workshare space, make sure it's one they're comfortable in.

Work and the Coronavirus

Since I wrote the above, many people around the world started working from home because of the coronavirus. Some call it the great equalizer because it attacks anyone, young or old, rich or poor, straight or gay. But the virus has actually amplified the inequities in our society. We are in this together, but we are not equal. Take time to think about that statement.

1. It wasn't expected, and it left people confused and dazed because nobody knew much about it.

2. Companies weren't prepared for this magnitude of work disruption.

3. Many companies didn't properly protect their employees.

4. When the official shutdown and shelter-at-home orders came from the government, many employees weren't prepared to work from home.

5. Many companies didn't communicate next steps with their employees.

6. Many companies didn't have enough information to relate to their employees.

7. Many companies didn't communicate for days, weeks, or more.

8. When communication was forthcoming, employees still felt left in the dark.

9. Many employees kept their jobs and began to work from home, but many were furloughed or let go.

10. Many companies were slow to communicate on how to handle benefits, 401(k)s, insurance, and flex pay; company credit cards were cut off.

11. Employees felt alone and abandoned by the companies they had put their faith in. As one person said, "So much for family."

The Future

I can go on and on about what should have happened, but that would be like playing quarterback when the game is over. Over in the sense that many companies are going to need to work hard to regain the trust of their employees. The ones who were let go and will be brought back, the ones who worked without proper protective gear. The ones who worked from home and had to juggle work and families, computers and cell phones.

The virus didn't feel like an equalizer when you were at home on a video call and didn't want your colleagues to see where and how you lived. It didn't feel like an equalizer when you weren't allowed to take your company laptop home and had to share with your home-schooled kids. It didn't feel like an equalizer when you and your partner and your kids were all huddled in a small space with no privacy. It was not an equalizer when you or your partner no longer had healthcare.

An upper management team at one company told staff to live off their savings. Guess what. Many didn't have savings they could live off, and many didn't have the option to get away to their weekend homes.

I mention these moments because they will not be forgotten when it's time to go back to work. As leaders, are you ready to rebuild your company culture in the moment that we'll be living in? This virus touched some people personally – they were sick, or someone they knew was sick, or someone they knew died. Some were mentally or physically abused. People will come back bruised, and if they don't show it on day one it will eventually surface. How do you build an authentic company culture after a national crisis?

By the time this book is published we will hopefully have come out on the other side of the pandemic. But questions above will still be important because as leaders you'll need to think about how you'll handle such an incident in the future – you'll need to think about what you could have done differently. I won't say better, just differently.

Chasing the Money

The coronavirus has not only affected the United States, it has affected the world. It has affected travel, trade, consumers, workers. It has affected every part of people's work lives and personal lives.

How will companies react? Some companies started making plans for remote work and separate offices early on. Some made it possible for their employees to apply for unemployment insurance with the hope that their business would survive and employees would get their jobs back.

Then you have the other CEOs and businesses, the ones who stayed open in order to chase the money.

Story Time

Allow me to share two stories that were told to me. The first is from a person in charge of infection control in an orthodontist's office. As the CDC was closing businesses and advising people to prepare for the unknown, the orthodontist (the CEO and a white man) refused to have a conversation with his fifteen employees. They asked to discuss the situation but he kept putting them off. When he finally called a staff meeting, he told his employees that all of them would catch the virus anyway, that it wasn't a big deal, and that they needed to keep working because his obligation was to his patients.

At the next meeting the staff told the CEO that his response wasn't good enough. He told them that if they didn't feel safe, they should quit and collect unemployment. When the staff asked if they would still have jobs when things settled down, the CEO said nothing.

The final meeting took place during the second week of working. *Keep in mind that the employees were working in people's mouths!* The person in charge of infection control asked what the policy was if a patient arrived sick. The CEO said to do the same as always. Of course, a patient did arrive who was sick – the CEO said nothing and didn't send them away.

He finally decided to close the office for two weeks after the American Association of Orthodontists said that no one should be working. (Notice that the CEO hadn't listened to the state government or the CDC, but he listened to an association.) He told the staff that they would be off for two weeks without pay. He never thanked them.

They were called back to work after two weeks and then furloughed because patients didn't keep their appointments.

What was the company culture before everything turned upside down? As this story was told to me, I heard mistrust, no respect, hints of shady practices, and bias. If these things are brewing in your company before something shakes your world, they'll burst through loud and clear afterward and will show what type of leader you are and your true company culture.

This orthodontist's office had a mix of clients, some wealthy and some on government assistance. The staff said that he treated the wealthy patients with time, attention, and care, while others were worked on by assistants, with the CEO doing a flyby check.

The staff was African American and Hispanic. Since he hired a diverse staff, they were surprised by the difference in care offered to different patients.

His staff felt mistrust and little respect for him. They knew before the pandemic that he didn't care about them, but the pandemic really brought it home to them that he didn't care about their health or their families' health. He hardly communicated with them, and when he did, he was focused on his bottom line. He wanted to make as much money as he could before he was forced to close.

The crazy thing is that some of his staff said that if he had just thanked them, they would feel differently about him.

I wish this leader luck in the coming weeks because he'll need to deal with people who are sitting in their feelings about him. A company lunch or dinner isn't going to smooth this over!

———

The day before New York, New Jersey, and Connecticut were told that 75 percent of their workforce had to stay home, I shared the following post:

> I'm in awe of how some companies have taken care of all of their employees and disgusted by the lack of concern of others. Do not be surprised

PAY ATTENTION
TO HOW COMPANIES
TREAT THEIR
EMPLOYEES
DURING THIS TIME

IT SPEAKS
VOLUMES
TO THEIR CORE ETHICS

how some workers return back to work, if they
return.

Email, text, and direct messages sent to me were wild
with stories. People in government said they were sent
home and told to take their laptops and that they would
continue to receive their pay. After being home only
one day, they were told to keep working but that they
wouldn't get paid. No reasons were given. They were
just told to keep working and it would be worked out.

At one private company workers stopped seeing
the leadership team. Why? Because the "team" had
taken their laptops and gone home or to their vacation homes. The rest of the workers, about fifteen of
them, were told that they had to come into the office
(after all, they didn't have laptops and weren't allowed
to use their personal computers). They were also told
that they were to cut back to two or three days a week,
that they wouldn't be fired, and that if they quit they
couldn't get unemployment.

———

I've heard far too many stories like these, stories about
nervous, unhappy, disappointed employees whose
leaders had failed them.

REMEMBER

Does everyone feel like they're included when they walk into work each day?

How you respond matters!

Company culture has feelings attached to it.

SPEAK UP ABOUT

DIVERSITY & INCLUSION

CHAPTER 11

Be the Ripple in the Pond of Change

CHANGE IS HARD. People love to talk about it, but *making it happen* is something different. You need your shareholders, board, and leadership to buy into it before you can even think about how it will affect employees.

That's why most people say, "I would love to change, but . . ." as an excuse to not act.

Stop Making Excuses and Stand Up!

Be the person who:

- Stands up and says that we can make changes that will be sustainable today as we work on the bigger policy changes

- Speaks up and recognizes that our company lacks diversity, inclusion, and an authentic company culture

- Has plans and takes the lead on developing how to fill in what's missing

- Is a champion, advocate, ally, or mentor
- Is not the savior of anyone
- Is supportive of what you may not understand
- Takes the time to learn so you can share what you have learned
- Is disruptive
- Is open to and awards diversity of thinking
- Is strategic
- Is accountable
- Is respectful
- Sparks conversations
- Acknowledges bias
- Brings in people who can discuss race, gender, leadership, disabilities, LGBTQ+
- Leads (if you are part of leadership)
- Examines the traditional ways to see if they're truly beneficial in the world we live in today
- Is the tsunami of change (departments, leaders, managers, culture, hiring, staff, vendors, programming, branding, board members)
- Brings up current events and how they affect the business and employees
- Is one who sees color but doesn't judge color (if you say you don't see color then you can't deal with issues of color, and it also means that you have no respect for my full self.)

- Doesn't pretend that issues will go away
- Is proactive
- Is a visionary
- Brings in a conflict coach for yourself, leadership, and employees
- Celebrates it when it's right!
- Changes it when it's not right!
- Uses your privilege – which allows you to say and do things others cannot say or do – for *good!*
- Doesn't need to have all the answers, but is open to hear the questions and alternative solutions
- Does your best to get the answers and share them
- Stops grouping Them together and thinking that They all feel the same way
- Says in the meeting, "Let's not group Them all together."
- Brings up the difference between race, racist, and racism (which are not only about white and black)
- Educates yourself on different cultures by reading, watching films, and taking the time to invest in understanding, and then asking questions.
- Knows that one of anything does not make you diverse
- Knows that white women cannot be the face of diversity, and that's OK

- Figures out how you can make a difference and not settle or accept what is or what was

If it's not your company, you can still be the ripple of change because you can speak up, and when you speak up have suggestions! If you're lucky you can even be backed up by other leaders. Many people have been solo acts for change!

Sometimes the change-makers are called whistleblowers; some of them are called CEOs; most are called leaders!

———

Being a leader has nothing to do with your actual title – it has to do with your actions!

———

———

Being a leader isn't about the department you lead – it's about the people you lead!

———

———

Be the ripple of change for yourself and others!

———

BECAUSE
MY GOOD
DOESN'T LOOK LIKE
YOUR GOOD

DOESN'T MEAN IT'S
NO GOOD

CHAPTER 12

It's Not Always About You

J UST CALL IT WHAT IT IS and stop beating around the bush.

If you're speaking about women, say *women*. If you're using *women* as a code word for *white women*, then say *white women* (of course you can't really say that because you don't want to be labeled a racist for not including black women, etc.). If the conversation is about race, then let's discuss race. If it's about disabilities, then say so. With LGBTQ+, each letter is a different conversation. Whatever you're speaking about be direct – don't beat about the bush.

Gender, race, disability, and LGBTQ+ may not look and sound the way you want them to. But just because they don't sit well with you doesn't mean they're not good. It doesn't mean that you can just discard people. It doesn't mean that you can just tolerate them – again, no one wants to just be tolerated.

Story Time

Labels

I moved into my first boarding house in New York City when I was 15. I was on scholarship with the Joffrey Ballet. There were 80 girls living there – models, dancers, some in school, some in fashion . . .

My parents dropped me off and I put my room in order and decided to go to the library area since it was a weekend and that's where many of the girls were hanging out. Of course, the dancers were on the floor stretching.

There was only one other black girl in the house. So needless to say the others stared at me, and then the questions came: "Why are you here?" I responded, "Why are you here?" The other girl said, "I'm on scholarship with the American Ballet." I said, "I'm on scholarship with the Joffrey Ballet" (yes, we did compete, it's a dancer thing). I was invited to join them on the floor, so I took a seat. I knew that more questions would come: "Is this your first time living here?" "Is this your first year at Joffrey?" "Have you performed professionally before?" Then I was told to not speak to that girl over there because girls on scholarship don't speak to girls not on scholarship because they're clearly not as good. I'm thinking, oh, now I'm a We.

As I stood up I made it clear that I speak to everyone.

I didn't look like them, but they wanted to make me a We because I was on scholarship, not because they knew me. They could tolerate me because I was close enough to be good enough for them.

They thought the other girl wasn't worthy because she wasn't on scholarship. But her good was good enough for me because she had every right to be there, as did everyone else. Just because she wasn't on scholarship didn't mean she couldn't dance rings around us. We didn't know why she wasn't on scholarship, so how could we judge her?

But those girls had a box they wanted to check off. Whether that girl was worthy of them saying hello to was about them, not about her. We all need to move past what we see and what we think we know and stop labeling people.

Bias

I worked at Macy's as a special events manager. I was working on an event with a well-known white male designer. His staff told me that they had an opening on their event team, and that they really liked me and the way I worked, but the designer only wanted blonds on his team. I just looked at her and said, "Well thanks for the compliment, I think, and it's his loss, not mine. "

In the first story the person was judged even though people didn't know her. In this one, the person was known, but the bias of race was stronger than the appreciation of talent.

Privilege

A preacher dressed like a homeless person and went to his church and took a seat. Most of his congregation moved away from him. He slowly stood up, and people yelled for someone to escort him out, until he went to the pulpit and they realized he was their preacher. He was saddened by their reaction and by how they treated someone they felt wasn't as privileged, clean, or sophisticated as they thought they were.

My good doesn't need to wear the same outfit as your good in order to be able to share the same message.

Part of looking at others as if they're not good enough is *privilege*, privilege of:

- Color
- Nationality
- Age
- Size
- School
- Ancestor
- Zip code
- Housing
- Clothing
- Appearance
- Title
- Clubs and Memberships
- Money
- Health

Here's the thing about privilege – it *can* be used for good. Let me repeat that: *privilege can be used for good.*

I've been in several meetings where leadership stated that they recognized that their whiteness was a privilege, and they felt that they could only be involved in Diversity and Inclusion decisions to a certain extent because they were white men. That may be partially true. But the truth is that your privilege of title can help push through what's needed. Your privilege may be the voice we need to help us be heard. Don't use your privilege as an excuse for not looking. Don't use your privilege as an easy out of situations that make you uncomfortable. Use your privilege for good. We need you!

What you don't know may make you uncomfortable. So what?!

More Stories

I've been asked to share the following stories given to me by others, and I think they belong in this chapter.

Food

Some companies have a kitchen or lounge area for lunch or breaks. When someone heats food the smell can linger, which is pleasant for some but not for others. The issue is the smell of the food, which is cultural. Employees shouldn't fear that they'll be ridiculed for bringing in the foods they're accustomed to eating and enjoying.

Why is your sandwich better than someone else's lunch?

Disabilities

A team of disabled athletes was flying to a tournament. They had fulfilled all the requirements necessary for a large group and for those with disabilities. They called ahead and said how many players and coaches would be traveling, along with the number of wheelchairs and able-bodied travelers. They asked for the normal assistance provided for those with disabilities, along with aisle chairs and chair tags.

If you're in a chair, you want to stay in your chair until it's time to board because the chair is your legs. It gives you the freedom to go to the restroom, get food, have a drink – the same things that able-bodied people do.

When it's time to board, you're lifted from your own chair to the aisle chair. Your chair is then supposed to be folded and placed under the plane with the proper tags so that if you have a connection, your chair is put on the connecting flight, or if you're at your final destination, your chair is at the gate. Once you're in your seat, the aisle chair is taken off the plane. You have no way to go to the restroom until the plane lands and you get your chair back (if you get it back).

In this instance, somewhere along the line someone decided to take the wheels off the chairs. So the team members were between flights with no chairs because the aisle chairs were only to get them on and off the plane (more on that in a moment). So there were ten athletes unable to do anything and people trying to figure out what wheels went on what chair. And no one wanted to take responsibility.

I unfortunately advised them first to go on Twitter and tag the airline. The airline responded but brushed them off with an offer for vouchers. The team wasn't happy about the vouchers, so I advised them to reach out again and direct message the airline. I also advised them to file an ADA complaint with the federal government because this wasn't the first time that this airline damaged wheelchairs and had issues with the disabled community. This story is still unsettled as I write this.

What makes you with your legs better then someone in a chair? And why are your bodily functions more important? The good of the disability community (the ones you see and the ones you don't see) may look different from yours, but that doesn't mean that your good is better or more important than theirs!

Affecting Others

What I do affects others as well as me. My good may look different from your good, but it isn't better, it's just different. How you move in this world, and how you act and react, can, and most likely will, determine how others can move in this world.

———

It's not always about you.

Before you decide if something is as good as you would like it to be, think about how it affects those it's supposed to be good for.
And think about whether their good works for them, not you.

———

Conclusion

There's a lot to be done across the globe. No matter where you live and work, Diversity and Inclusion is important and shouldn't be thought of as add-ons or a trend. It's hard, it takes work, and we need all voices involved to make change.

———

Be the change, make a difference, be a champion and an advocate, and work your way toward being an ally.

———

Global Diversity and Inclusion Efforts

GLOBALLY, Diversity and Inclusion is still focused on gender (women) and disabilities.

In the United States, we focus on diversity of race, then gender. But in the last few years I've noticed that there's a newly focused effort on gender. White females first, then maybe others.

In the United States we speak about race, gender, and LGBTQ+, and then disabilities and veterans.

The European Union

Global companies are now realizing that they too must open their doors to those who may not look like them or have the same accent, but who are qualified to do the work. In late 2019, a new Diversity and Inclusion Charter was sent out by the European Commission, the executive branch of the European Union.

Check out: bit.ly/EU-DI-Charter

Individual EU countries have their own diversity charters that companies in the country can sign committing them to promoting diversity and equal opportunities for their staffs. Thousands of companies have signed on.

Check out: bit.ly/EU-DI-Country-Charters

Israel

The Israel Equal Employment Opportunities Commission's Diversity Initiative, a voluntary partnership with participating companies, was launched in 2017. Rather than an obligatory reporting approach, the commission and the firms in the program embark together on a three-year process advancing Diversity and Inclusion; this period entails eighteen months of close monitoring by a commission team and organizational consultants it provides.

During the first eighteen months, the commission and consultants examine the organization's quantitative variables. This includes analysis of the extent to which diverse groups are represented in a range of classifications and ranks; study of the existing organizational culture takes place through interviews with managers and employees. Subsequent to this phase, which includes a comprehensive examination report, the parties consolidate a joint diversity plan entailing both quantitative and qualitative goals; implementation proceeds following approval. The team forms a steering committee that monitors the process; the committee observes managers and employees – including human resources recruiters – and also carries out training sessions, in accordance with the working plan.

The process is completed after eighteen months (unless extended as per mutual agreement); at this juncture, an assessment is made in accordance with the predetermined benchmarks. From this point onward, monitoring of the organization takes place at a distance to ensure that diversity management continues as a matter of routine. The commission remains available to the organization for consultation and guidance to the extent necessary.

— The Israel Equal Employment Opportunities Commission (EEOC)

I was amazed how much the country gets involved with companies. It's great to think about it. If you take money from the country, then the country needs to ensure that all employees are treated equitably.

Check out the latest diversity report from Israel: bit.ly/Israel-DI

Global Recap

Global Diversity and Inclusion strategies focus on four main target groups: women, staff with disabilities, LGBTQ+, and older staff. Notice that there's very little to nothing about race. On the flip side, the United States has just begun to speak about ageism as part of Diversity and Inclusion.

Diversity and Inclusion Monthly Calendar

UNDERSTAND *WHY*

YOU DO
THE THINGS
YOU DO

JANUARY

What's In Your Bag?

What's in your bag that can make you a good leader?

1.
2.
3.
4.
5.
6.
7.

What's in your bag that you need to work on to make you a better leader?

1.
2.
3.
4.
5.
6.
7.
8.
9.
10.

WHAT DOES *DIVERSITY* *&INCLUSION* MEAN TO YOU?

TO YOUR COMPANY?

FEBRUARY

Does Diversity and Inclusion Matter to You?
To Your Company?

What does diversity mean to you?

What does inclusion mean to you?

What does diversity mean to your company?

What does inclusion mean to your company?

What can you do to improve your Diversity and Inclusion efforts?

THERE'S MORE TO DIVERSITY & INCLUSION THAN CHECKED BOXES

MARCH

Checked Boxes Aren't Good Enough!

How does your company check the boxes and how can you make a change?

1.

2.

3.

4.

5.

6.

7.

8.

9.

10.

DIVERSITY
& INCLUSION
SHOULD BE A PROMISE WITH
EXECUTION
NOT
A PROBLEM
AND A PROMISE

APRIL

With Diversity and Inclusion Comes Responsibility

How are you going to move from promises to execution?

1. _____

2. _____

3. _____

4. _____

5. _____

6. _____

7. _____

8. _____

9. _____

10. _____

STOP
FAKING IT
HOPING YOU WON'T GET CAUGHT

MAY

Aspiration vs. Operation

Connect the dots so that your company isn't just about aspiration but also about operation. How will you stop faking it till you make it?

1. _____

2. _____

3. _____

4. _____

5. _____

6. _____

7. _____

8. _____

9. _____

10. _____

THINK
ABOUT
PEOPLE

JUNE
It's Time to Think Differently!

What will you change your mindset about?

1. _____

2. _____

3. _____

4. _____

5. _____

6. _____

7. _____

8. _____

9. _____

10. _____

AVOID
SILOS

JULY

Diversity and Inclusion Should Not Be Built in Silos

How can you change the way you work and ensure that inclusion doesn't turn into silos?

1. _____

2. _____

3. _____

4. _____

5. _____

6. _____

7. _____

8. _____

9. _____

10. _____

MAKE SURE
THAT THE PEOPLE
IN THE ROOM
LOOK LIKE
THE PEOPLE
YOU'RE TRYING TO
REACH

AUGUST

Nothing About Us Without Us!

Ensure that the following people or departments will be involved at the beginning of a project and will be invited to meetings.

1. _____

2. _____

3. _____

4. _____

5. _____

6. _____

7. _____

8. _____

9. _____

10. _____

IF YOU AREN'T COMMITTED TO THE WORK,

DON'T SAY YOU ARE DOING THE WORK

SEPTEMBER

Be Committed to the Work

If you're serious about commitment, what are you doing to commit?

1.

2.

3.

4.

5.

6.

7.

8.

9.

10.

CULTURE
IS NOT SOMETHING YOU
SPEAK ABOUT

IT'S SOMETHING YOU
CREATE

OCTOBER

Create an Authentic Company Culture

How can you improve your company culture? (It can always improve.)

1. _____

2. _____

3. _____

4. _____

5. _____

6. _____

7. _____

8. _____

9. _____

10. _____

SPEAK UP ABOUT DIVERSITY & INCLUSION

NOVEMBER

Be the Ripple in the Pond of Change

You will stand up and be an advocate, ally, or champion for what and for whom?

1. _____

2. _____

3. _____

4. _____

5. _____

6. _____

7. _____

8. _____

9. _____

10. _____

BECAUSE
MY GOOD
DOESN'T LOOK LIKE
YOUR GOOD

DOESN'T MEAN IT'S
NO GOOD

DECEMBER
It's Not All About You

How will you review your biases, recognize them, and work to change them for yourself and the company?

1.

2.

3.

4.

5.

6.

7.

8.

9.

10.

> "THE OCEAN DOES NOT APOLOGIZE FOR ITS DEPTH, AND THE MOUNTAINS DO NOT SEEK FORGIVENESS FOR THE SPACE THEY TAKE, AND SO, NEITHER SHALL I"

— BECCA LEE

APPENDIX C

Facing Race and Racism During a Global Pandemic

I CELEBRATED TURNING IN MY MANUSCRIPT to the publisher before my due date. Whoo-hoo! But let's be honest – we were in the midst of the coronavirus pandemic and I had nowhere to go and nothing to do but be at home and finish the book.

I shared with you in past chapters how companies and leadership handled the beginning of the pandemic. But I felt that I needed to do a quick update to share what's happened almost two months into being told to work from home.

Businesses had to close unless they were classified as essential. Many offices needed to furlough employees, and the lucky ones that didn't have to let employees go had their employees work from home, or they received PPE/PPP loans to help them bring employees back to work. But for how long? That was the question on employees' minds.

This is where things became shaky. Employees who were never considered essential became essential, and all of a sudden they were expected to show up or they would lose their jobs. They were now putting themselves as well as their families in jeopardy of falling ill or worse. Most were left with no option but to show up and suck it up.

Leadership, as we've talked about earlier, didn't always do the best job of communicating. Granted, how long the pandemic would last was anyone's guess, and the scramble to work from home, and figuring out how you would work from home when the entire family was at home, was a challenge at the beginning and has stayed a challenge.

An additional challenge arose when many leaders didn't uphold their company culture and code-of-conduct rules. Leaders told women to wear make-up for video calls, yet men showed up with their hair uncombed, in pajama tops, no bottoms. . . . I agree that you should look presentable on video, but telling women to put on makeup, and having a different standard for men, is unacceptable.

Black employees and employees of color felt left out of many meetings, meetings they would have been part of in the office, because they weren't invited by their colleagues. They were told that they'd be updated and were given orders to go do the work. They were left out of decision-making.

There were employees who felt that they weren't being protected from racist, biased, xenophobic, homophobic, and offensive language used not only by other employees but also by leadership on virtual calls and in emails. Where were leadership, HR, and Diversity and

Inclusion leaders? They were cutting budgets and dismantling their Diversity and Inclusion departments. I'll come back to that in a moment.

While the world was upside down some companies thought that it was a great idea to do mass firing via video. No advance calls, no emails, no follow up. Employees received invitations to join email meetings, only to be told that they were being let go. Leadership forgot that people share when things are good, but they record and share when things are bad.

Who thought that firing everyone online was a great idea? And where was the rest of the leadership team? If you were part of the leadership who couldn't be bothered to call your employees individually to let them go, in the midst of a pandemic, then you're part of the problem, not part of the solution.

Leadership is more than a title. Office politics be damned. Stand Up!

Let's circle back to the cutting of budgets. In the past the marketing and public relations budgets were usually the first to be cut. This time around, many Diversity and Inclusion departments were reassigned or dismantled. I pointed out to one CEO that she needed to make an effort to diversify her company, and someone needed to make sure that effort happened. Who would be responsible? Blank stare and silence.

No one wanted to make a commitment to examine their Diversity and Inclusion efforts and no one was willing to adjust them. This is not the time to dismantle D&I departments, this is not the time to rename them "Belonging" departments. We were all together in the pandemic, but we were not equal in the pandemic – blacks and people of color were affected very differently from whites in the numbers getting sick and the numbers dying.

Because so many employees felt that their concerns about working from home, health issues, along with Diversity and Inclusion issues were not being heard, I started a webinar that's held on Wednesday evenings. I thought I would do a three-part series, but it's turned into a weekly series and podcast called Visibility Ultd., with a global audience. I've heard from everyone under the Diversity and Inclusion umbrella and those looking for new solutions to old problems – gender, race, LG-BTQ+, and those with disabilities seen and unseen.

Employees want to be heard, they want to feel like they're adding value to their company and that the company is adding value to their lives outside of a paycheck (social responsibility). Those with disabilities want to know what excuse they'll be given for not getting hired now, since clearly many people can work from home.

Racism in America and at Work

I accepted several online (unpaid) speaking engagements during the pandemic to make sure that Diversity and Inclusion stay top of mind. The world takes one more turn and lands on racism. We watched a black man get shot and killed while jogging (Ahmaud Arbery), a black women get shot and killed in her home while sleeping (Breonna Taylor), and the murder of George Floyd – one more black man saying "I can't breathe."

We're only allowed thirty hashtags on Instagram, not enough for all the black people who have been killed at the hands of white America for doing everyday tasks.

Watching George Floyd being murdered on TV blew the lid off the pot of racism in America. Nothing that black America didn't already know. My phone and email exploded – what do we do, we need a statement, who do we give money to?

I'm a black women who's never felt the need to say, "I'm a black woman." Now I'm online with companies that have ten to thousands of employees, and I have to say, "I'm a black woman and here's why you need to say that Black Lives Matter." This is not the moment to refer to *people of color*.

Saying *people of color* is a way for white people to feel comfortable. We are black and brown and many other shades, but the conversation at this moment is about Black Lives Matter. It's not that other lives don't matter, but at this moment we need to speak about Black Lives Matter. No buts, no maybes, no All Lives Matter, no "I don't see color." No. We need you to just listen about Black Lives Matter and why they matter and why it matters to your company.

I've been told that the Black Lives Matter organization has said some negative things. My black life has nothing to do with an organization. If you can only see an organization, that's part of the problem.

The companies I've worked with said they needed help. They didn't want to misstep and they didn't want to be silent. They knew they had not honestly thought about black lives and how their employees must be feeling. These companies were honest in saying that they didn't want to jump into a conversation they weren't part of to begin with. So, we crafted a statement that stayed true to brand and recognized their shortcomings, and had them commit to sustainable, accountable *action*, not just promises.

I was also hired to conduct a town hall meeting. I respected the CEOs I've worked with for being aware that they weren't the best choice to speak to staff when the discussion needed to be about race. Each CEO spoke briefly, then turned the meeting over to me to explain and discuss bias, race, racism, and racists, and why the conversation is needed, not just for a day but moving forward, continuing the conversation and reviewing all the touch points within the company.

In addition to the staff members who worked with me on the statement, I had access to sales teams, marketing, and leadership. The CEO said, let's do this right.

A week before, these departments weren't important, and now I had the opportunity to say, "I will be holding you accountable for the commitments you're making. Black people will hold you accountable. The world will hold you accountable. Each of you in the company will need to hold the others accountable. And while you're holding yourself accountable you need to take care of your black employees. They're not OK, and they haven't been OK for some time. We've watched a man be killed and then we've watched the world finally say it's wrong. We've been saying that there's an injustice, there's a price to pay for being black in America, for being black at work, for being black walking down the street, and for being black at home. We're judged on who we are by the color of our skin, not by our talents. We are a checked box for some and a prop for others."

I don't condone the looting of stores. Some of you who are reading this book may have lost stores and product. I don't agree with tearing things apart. But if the silent protests of the past and present haven't worked, why has the rioting finally made people see that Black Lives Matter? What is it that makes you act when other people don't act?

Take the time to go back to Chapter 1, "What's In Your Bag?"

I look forward to the changes that I see taking place, but the changes can't be in the heat of the moment. This isn't the time for knee-jerk reactions, it's not the time to put out statements, add black boxes, or act like you understand Juneteenth. This is the time to do a full review of your company, from the photos on your website to your diversity statement. The mailroom, the boardroom, and every suite and non-suite in between need to be reviewed.

I'm hopeful when I see companies take a stand when one of their employees makes racist remarks, or uses the race card to call the police, or goes off on a black person for no valid reason. Now people pay the price of losing their jobs if what they've done is caught on tape.

I've been asked if I think that companies are scared of bad publicity. Of course they are. No company wants to be dragged through the press for race issues. In the climate we're in, and I hope we stay in, we can honestly look at each situation and hold the company and its employees accountable for their actions.

Between the pandemic and the heightened spotlight on race, racism, and Diversity and Inclusion, this is the time to update your handbooks. This is not the time to dismantle your Diversity and Inclusion department, regardless of where your company is located.

The conversation on race isn't the same as the conversation on Diversity and Inclusion. You don't create a department for black people, you create a Diversity and Inclusion department to assure that people of any race or gender, people with disabilities, or members of the LGBTQ+ community, have the same opportunities within the company as those who are not under the D&I umbrella. You cannot create a Diversity and Inclusion department June 14, 2020, without having a conversation on race. Bias can be part of the conversation, but an honest, open conversation on race is needed. More than one conversation is needed, and training is needed. If we could have "fixed" the race issue in a one-hour webinar, don't you think we would have done so by now?

The only time outside of a national holiday when all fifty states have accomplished anything together is when people vote! Peaceful protests took place in all fifty states and all over the world. Let's turn our protests into action by voting.

You as a leader, as a company owner, regardless of your company's size, must look within to see how you can improve inclusion within your company. Don't call it belonging – *belonging* and *inclusion* are two different words. For clarity: You *belong* to a group. *Inclusion* is having the feeling that you're valued within the group.

Once you've looked within you can begin to build strong, sustainable outreach to the black communities and other communities that you haven't been authentically speaking to. This outreach will be bigger than events and advertising; it will be a commitment to diversity for your leadership, your C-suites, your directors, your board, and your entire company.

Nothing About Us Without Us!

Let's Make Change Together

If you would like to view my webinars check them out on YouTube:

The Cavu Group: bit.ly/Leslie-Short-Webinars

or via podcast on all major listening options:

Visibility Ultd.: anchor.fm/leslie-short

I hope I'm opening a door to real conversation about race and bias in the workplace. The conversations must continue, whether online or when we return to the "new" office. Company culture and race will need to be discussed. I also hope that by the time this book comes out my prediction that companies will bring in mental health counselors, grief counselors, and Diversity and Inclusion speakers and trainers, who can speak from experience as well as knowledge, will have come true.

For now, we work from home. Working from home or online doesn't alter the fact that change is happening now, from the streets to the boardroom. The race conversation is not going away, so prepare for it. And don't prepare for it by asking your black employees to explain it you – it's not their responsibility. Hire the experts and do your research. Don't try to be the savior – be part of the solution. Use your privilege of position to encourage the changes. Remember that it's not about you, it's about turning They & Them into We & Us.

Be the Ripple in the Pond of Change: Reread Chapter 11.

ABOUT THE AUTHOR

Leslie Short brings four decades of experience to The Cavu Group to advise companies and organizations on how to expand beyond their current culture through the Diversity and Inclusion lens. This is an effort to facilitate and create new solutions to old and new issues.

Leslie's talents and skills are uniquely designed to seek growth through open conversations, conflict coaching, trainings, and workshops. She firmly believes that issues don't go away because programs are in place; they go away when an organization continually evolves and has a channel to listen and understand the people who are its greatest assets. Leslie has been developing multi-cultural/mosaic marketing, programming, and opportunities as far back as 1998.

Leslie began her career as a classical ballet dancer at the age of seven, turning professional at twelve. She expanded her career in Paris, living in Europe for over ten years and Asia for three. She was Creator and CEO of the first-of-its-kind entertainment business in Japan, rated best business of Japan in 1994. She spent the next stage of her career leading production of television, media & entertainment, and fashion projects.

She went on to become the COO and Corporate Operations Strategist for celebrities and companies including ABC Shark Tank Founder Daymond John and his companies FUBU the Collection, FB Entertainment, The Shark Group, and blueprint + co. As CEO she launched K.I.M. Media (Keep it Moving) and founded Ascend Bereavement Management.

Leslie is also a chaplain, activist, certified mental health aide, certified mediator, and conflict/transformative coach, as well as a dignitary and keynote speaker at United Nations and European Union events around the world.

Leslie has been developing multi-cultural/mosaic business innovation models and ecosystems that thrive over the span of her career. In addition to being an active leader in New York's business community, she's an award-winning speaker and has been recognized for her achievements by various organizations. In 2003 she was honored by *Ebony* as an Outstanding Woman in Marketing & Communications, and by *Today's Black Woman Magazine* with the Today's Black Woman and New Day Associates Award. Leslie was selected as a "Woman of Influence" by the *New York Business Journal* for 2016, and she is a member of the North American Advisory board for the CMO (Chief Marketing Officer) Council. Leslie also authored a chapter of *Inside the Minds: Marketing Benchmarks for Success*, with Aspatore Books, and contributed her insights to the college textbooks *Marketing, 9th Edition* and *Marketing: The Core 3rd Edition*. She was a Forbes.com Black Women To Watch in 2019 and 2020.

www.ingramcontent.com/pod-product-compliance
Lightning Source LLC
Chambersburg PA
CBHW071212210326
41597CB00016B/1778